U.S. Forces in the Middle East

CSIS Middle East Dynamic Net Assessment

U.S. Forces in the Middle East

Resources and Capabilities

Anthony H. Cordesman

WestviewPress

A Division of HarperCollins*Publishers*

Published in 1997 in the United States of America by Westview Press, 5500 Central Avenue, Boulder, Colorado 80301, and in the United Kingdom by Westview Press, 12 Hid's Copse Road, Cumnor Hill, Oxford OX2 9JJ

Library of Congress Cataloging-in-Publication Data
Cordesman, Anthony H.
    US forces in the Middle East : resources and capabilities /
Anthony H. Cordesman
        p.   cm.
    Includes bibliographical references.
    ISBN 0-8133-3245-1 (hc). — ISBN 0-8133-3246-X (pbk)
    1. United States—Military policy.   2. United States—Armed
Forces—Middle East.   I. Title.
UA23.C67374   1997
355'.031'09730536—dc21   96-46615
                                                                                     CIP

This book was typeset by Letra Libre, 1705 Fourteenth Street, Suite 391, Boulder, Colorado 80302.

The paper used in this publication meets the requirements of the American National Standard for Permanence of Paper for Printed Library Materials Z39.48-1984.

10   9   8   7   6   5   4   3   2   1

Contents

Tables and Illustrations

Charts

Maps

Preface

This volume is part of an ongoing dynamic net assessment of the Gulf. The project was conceived by David Abshire and Richard Fairbanks of the Center for Strategic and International Studies, and focuses on the foreign policy, military forces, politics, economics, energy sector, and internal security of each Gulf state, and US strategy and power projection capabilities in the Gulf. Separate volumes are available on Kuwait, Iran, Iraq, Saudi Arabia, and US forces. Bahrain, Oman, Qatar, and the UAE are combined into a single volume.

Each of these volumes is interlinked to provide comparable data on the current situation and trends in each country, and to portray the overall trends in key areas like the economy and the military balance. The volume on Iran provides a detailed graphic overview of the military trends in the region, but each volume shows how the key economic and military developments in each country relate to the developments in other Gulf countries.

At the same time, this series deliberately emphasizes nation-by-nation analysis. Iran and Iraq clearly deserve separate treatment. The Southern Gulf states are largely independent actors and are driven by separate strategic, political, economic, and military interests. In spite of the creation of the Arab Gulf Cooperation Council (GCC), there is little practical progress in strategic, economic, or military cooperation, and there are serious rivalries and differences of strategic interest between Bahrain, Kuwait, Oman, Qatar, Saudi Arabia, and the UAE. The Southern Gulf cannot be understood in terms of the rhetoric of the Arab Gulf Cooperation Council, or by assuming that developments in Bahrain, Kuwait, Oman, Qatar, Saudi Arabia, and the UAE are similar and these states have an identity of interest.

These Gulf studies are also part of a broader dynamic net assessment of the Middle East, and a separate study is available of the trends in the Arab-Israeli military balance and the peace process. See Anthony H. Cordesman, *Perilous Prospects*, Boulder, Westview, 1996.

Anthony H. Cordesman

Acknowledgments

This volume is part of a six-volume series reporting on a dynamic net assessment of the Gulf. The project was conceived by David Abshire and Richard Fairbanks of the Center for Strategic and International Studies, and is part of a broader dynamic net assessment of the entire Middle East.

The author would like to thank Kimberly Goddes and Kiyalan Batmanglidj for their research and editing help in writing this series, and Thomas Seidenstein and David Hayward for helping to edit each volume.

Many US and international analysts and agencies played a role in commenting on drafts of the manuscript. So did experts in each Southern Gulf country. The author cannot acknowledge these contributions by name or agency but he is deeply grateful. The author would also like to thank his colleagues at the CSIS who reviewed various manuscripts and commented on the analysis. These colleagues include Richard Fairbanks and Arnaud de Borchgrave, and his Co-Director of the Middle East Program, Judith Kipper.

A.H.C.

1

Introduction

The United States plays a vital strategic role in the Gulf. US military forces and power projection capabilities deter Iran and Iraq—two aggressive and radical regimes with military forces that might otherwise dominate the Gulf. The US prevents these states from achieving regional hegemony and intimidating their Southern Gulf neighbors. At the same time, the US plays a critical stabilizing role in the Southern Gulf, compensating in part for the lack of cooperation between the Gulf states and their internal rivalries. This strategic role affects a critical part of the world's energy supplies. The Gulf has at least 649 billion barrels of proven oil reserves out of the world's total proven reserves of 999.8 billion barrels, and 1,549 trillion cubic feet of gas out of a world total of 4,980 trillion cubic feet.[1]

Put differently, the Gulf has nearly 65% of the world's oil reserves and 33% of its gas reserves. Iran has 8.9%, Iraq has 10.0%, Kuwait has 9.7%, Qatar has 0.2%, Saudi Arabia has 26.1%, and the UAE has 9.8%. The West, other countries of the developed world, and virtually all developing states are critically dependent on the stable flow of energy resources out of the Gulf, and every major projection of world energy balances indicates that this dependence will increase steadily throughout the period between 1995 and 2025—the year where most such projections end.[2]

There is no question that US military capabilities in the Gulf are a critical measure of its ability to maintain the stability of the world's economy and global economic development and growth. However, analyzing the trends in US military capabilities in the Gulf is not a simple task. US capabilities in the Gulf are shaped by the size of the total pool of forces the US maintains on a world-wide basis. It is US capability to deploy given portions of this pool of forces to the Gulf to deal with a specific crisis that is critical, not the forces the US normally deploys forward or allocates to the US Central Command (USCENTCOM).

This means that US capabilities are scenario specific in the sense they will be shaped by the level of warning the US receives, the support it receives from its allies, its forward deployments at the start of a contingency, the speed with which the US can deploy its forces, US capability to sustain its forces once deployed, and the risk the US may have to commit forces to another region that it cannot deploy to the Gulf.

At the same time, US capabilities are not static, they change over time and will be shaped by the defense effort the US has made in the years before a crisis. They will also interact with the future capabilities of allied forces. This point is particularly important in view of the changes in American defense policy, strategy, and force levels since the break up of the Soviet Union and Warsaw Pact.

Much of this change in US military capability has been resource driven, as various Administrations and the Congress have cut American defense spending to levels far below the spending peaks of the Cold War. As a result of the actions of the Bush and Clinton Administrations, the US has adopted plans that are cutting US forces by at least 35%, relative to their level in FY1985. In spite of recent additions to the FY1996 defense budget by a Republican-controlled Congress, current Department of Defense plans still call for real defense expenditures to decline by at least 45% between FY1985–FY1997.[3]

However, any analysis of US capabilities in the Gulf must also be based on an analysis of the broader changes in US strategy, forces, and power projection capabilities that are reshaping US contingency capabilities. The present and future US capabilities in the Gulf cannot be analyzed solely in terms of "inputs." Military power is always a function of the ability to fight given types of conflict against a given enemy in a specific time and place. Power is a function of each side's strategic commitment, alliances, and the political factors that shape a conflict.

It is equally important to consider friendly and allied capabilities. US forces are unlikely to operate in a vacuum. The "tanker war" of 1987–1988, the Gulf War of 1990, the operation to protect the Kurds in Iraq, and the US build-up in Kuwait in 1994 have all shown that the US benefits from cooperation with its allies and is dependent upon such cooperation. Britain, Egypt, France, and Syria all provided significant support from outside the region during the Gulf War. Britain and France, however, are in the process of making much more serious force cuts than the US, and Syria's military efforts have declined sharply since 1990, while Egypt's military capabilities have improved. This makes it almost impossible to predict the level of external military forces that might support the US in a future crisis, and the future political intentions of outside states are equally uncertain.

In contrast, all six of the southern Gulf states—Bahrain, Kuwait, Oman, Qatar, Saudi Arabia, and the UAE—have established much stronger bilateral military relations with the US since the Gulf War. While they have many mutual rivalries, and have failed to strengthen their collective defense capabilities and make effective use of the military potential of the Gulf Cooperation Council (GCC), they are improving their separate national forces, and currently a high probability exists that they would support the US in any military contingency that threatened the Southern Gulf. Further, US capability to provide arms transfers and military training and assistance to the friendly states provides both local forces that can substitute for US capabilities and improved capabilities for coalition warfare. As a result, cooperative military agreements with the Southern Gulf states and arms transfers to these states comprise another important dimension of US capabilities in the Gulf.

At the same time, uncertainty will play a major role. It is impossible to predict the form a future war will take, or to explore all of the possible conflicts that can occur over time. Past experience has shown that it is valuable to consider capabilities for a major regional conflict with the most likely enemy or enemies, but history has also shown that no war is ever an exact repetition of the past or follows the predictions of military planners and strategic analysts. As a result, it is generally better to focus on broad military capabilities than examine all possible scenarios.

Finally, any analysis of US capabilities must consider the proliferation of weapons of mass destruction, and advanced weapons systems to deliver such weapons. It may not be possible to predict the rate at which Iran and Iraq will acquire such weapons, or their precise future war-fighting capabilities. It is already clear, however, that both states are committed to acquiring such war-fighting capabilities, and that US counterproliferation capabilities must now be considered as a key aspect of US military capabilities in the Gulf.

MAP ONE   The Gulf Region

2

Changes in US Defense Budgets, Strategy, and Force Plans

US capabilities in the Gulf are being shaped by a long series of changes in US defense budgets, strategy, and force plans that have taken place as a result of the end of the Cold War. While it is normal to discuss such changes beginning with strategy and force plans, the driving force has been the effort to reduce defense expenditures. Since the end of the Cold War, US strategy and forces have been driven more by the search for peace dividends rather than by strategic requirements and war fighting considerations.

At the same time, the Bush and Clinton Administrations have made important changes in strategy and force plans. These changes began under President Bush. In August, 1990, the Bush Administration presented a new future years defense plan (FYDP) called the "Base Force." The Base Force shifted the focus of US strategy from the Soviet Union and Warsaw Pact to a focus on power projection and the capability to fight major regional conflicts.

The Clinton Administration continued this focus, and made further cuts in defense spending. In September, 1993, it announced the results of a "Bottom Up Review" (BUR) that called for the US to reshape its forces to deal with two near simultaneous major regional conflicts—one in Korea and the other in the Southwest Asia. It also announced new force improvement packages to improve US power projection capabilities and new plans to deal with peace keeping and low-level conflicts.

The Impact of Cuts in Total US Defense Spending

The trends in US defense spending are best indicated by the trends in total annual defense budget authority—a measurement which covers all US defense expenditures authorized for both the current budget year and any future years.[4] Measured in constant FY1995 dollars, this spending reached a Reagan-era peak of $402.2 billion in FY1985. It then dropped to

$384.6 billion in FY1986, $370.3 billion in FY1987, $362.6 billion in FY1988, $357.7 billion in FY1989, $349.7 billion in FY1990, $314.58 billion in FY1991, $314.7 billion in FY1992, $289.3 billion in FY1993, $264.8 billion in FY1994, $263.5 billion in FY1995, $253.8 billion in FY1996, and $228 billion in FY1997.[5]

Table One and Chart One show the pace of these reductions since the Gulf War. They show that total Department of Defense budget authority in constant FY1997 dollars dropped from $352.6 billion in FY1990 to $242.6 billion in FY1997. During FY1990-FY1997, there were substantial cuts in real spending in five out of the eight budget years and only a minor increase in FY1992 to pay for the Gulf War.

These cuts in defense spending have produced a major "peace dividend." They not only have saved billions of dollars in military spending relative to the levels of the Cold War; they have interacted with the growth of the US economy to reduce defense spending as a share of both the GNP and federal budget. Defense spending dropped from 6.2% of the GNP in FY1985 to 3.7% in FY1995 and 3.2% in FY1997, and from 26.8% of all federal spending in FY1985 to 16.9% in FY1995 and 15% in FY1997.

These cuts have produced a 53% reduction in the burden that military spending places on the US economy, and a 44% reduction in the burden military spending places on the total federal budget.[6] This peace dividend is likely to continue to grow. The Department of Defense projects that defense spending will drop still further to 2.7% of the GNP in FY2002, and slightly less than 13.5% of the federal budget.[7]

At the same time, these cuts in defense spending have had an impact on US military capability that is severe enough to raise serious questions as to whether the US will retain the capabilities it needs to maintain its present role as a superpower and its ability to deal with possible threats in Southwest Asia. They raise questions as to whether the US can maintain the combat readiness, forward presence, and strategic mobility it needs for the range of contingencies it faces in the Gulf. And they raise questions as to whether the US can afford the modernization it needs to improve its forces and react to the lessons of the Gulf War.

US funding levels threatened to produce significant readiness problems as early as FY1995, and the Clinton Administration later acknowledged that the US defense program for FY1996–FY2001 was underfunded by at least $49 billion. President Clinton dealt with this situation by adding $25 billion (in the out years of the program), saving $12 billion by cutting estimates of inflation, and making a $12 billion reduction in modernization.

President Clinton's FY1996 budget request still, however, called for a 5.3% cut in real spending, and reduced total spending in budget authorizations to $246.0 billion. This meant a total cut in real defense spending

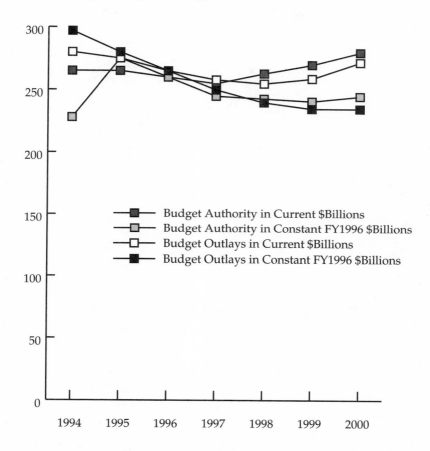

CHART ONE   Trends in US Department of Defense Spending: FY1994–FY2001 (in Current and Constant FY96 $Billions (050)). *Source:* OSD Comptroller.

of 39% between FY1985 and FY1996, and a cut of 33.9% since FY1990—the period just before the start of the Gulf War.[8] The Clinton Administration also proposed further cuts in budget authority during FY1997, FY1998, and FY1999, that would have cut real defense spending by 4.4% for a total of 43.4% since FY1995, and 38.3% since the Gulf War—with rises of a little over 1% occurring in FY2000 and FY2001. These plans would produce a cumulative cut in real defense budget authorizations of 9.9% between FY1994 and FY2001, and an 18.8% cut in real defense budget outlays.[9]

The Congress did not approve the Clinton FY1996 budget proposal, and added $7 billion to the President's request during its debate over the

TABLE ONE   Trends in US Department of Defense Spending: FY1990–FY1997

Category	FY90	FY91	FY92	FY93	FY94	FY95	FY96	FY97
In Constant US FY1997 $Billions								
Military Personnel	97.9	99.9	93.7	84.0	77.0	75.4	71.6	69.8
Operations & Maintenance	88.3	117.2	93.8	89.2	88.3	93.8	93.5	89.2
Procurement	81.4	71.7	63.0	52.8	44.1	53.6	42.3	38.9
Research, Development, Test, & Evaluation	36.5	36.2	36.6	38.0	34.6	34.5	34.9	34.8
Military Construction	5.1	5.2	5.3	4.6	6.0	5.4	6.9	5.3
Family Housing	3.1	3.3	3.7	3.9	3.5	3.4	4.3	3.9
Defense-wide Contingency	—	—	—	—	—	—	-0.6	-0.04
Revolving & Management Funds	0.6	2.7	4.6	4.5	4.4	5.3	1.8	1.7
Trust & Receipts	-0.8	-44.3	-5.7	-0.4	-0.8	-1.6	-0.5	-0.5
Deductions & Transfers	-0.03	-0.03	-0.6	-1.2	-0.1	-0.2	-0.4	-0.2
Total	293.0	276.2	281.9	267.4	251.6	255.7	251.8	242.6
% of Real Change								
Military Personnel	-1.0	2.1	-6.3	-10.4	-8.4	-2.1	-5.0	-2.5
Operations & Maintenance	-1.1	23.6	-20.5	-7.5	-3.5	4.5	-2.6	-7.0
Procurement	-0.8	-14.2	-14.2	-17.9	-18.1	-3.3	-5.0	-9.9
Research, Development, Test, & Evaluation	-6.5	-4.2	-1.4	1.5	-10.8	-2.1	-1.2	-2.5
Military Construction	-13.7	-1.6	-1.1	-15.1	29.2	-11.6	24.6	-25.4
Family Housing	-7.4	0.5	10.9	3.1	-13.0	-4.9	24.2	-12.3

(continues)

TABLE ONE   *(continued)*

Category	FY90	FY91	FY92	FY93	FY94	FY95	FY96	FY97
Defense-wide Contingency	—	—	—	—	—	—	—	—
Revolving & Management Funds	—	—	—	—	—	—	—	—
Trust & Receipts	—	—	—	—	—	—	—	—
Deductions & Transfers	—	—	—	—	—	—	—	—
Total	-2.2	-10.0	0.2	-7.9	-8.2	-0.3	-3.7	-6.0

Source: William J. Perry, *Annual Report to the President and the Congress, FY1997*, Washington, Department of Defense, 1996, p. B-1.

defense budget. At the same time, many of the Congressional add-ons to the FY-1996 budget were little more than "pork" and special interest funding. They allocated money to submarines, the B-2, and strategic missile defense in ways that created significant new spending obligations or "mortgages" in future years. As a result, the Congressional add-ons had the net effect of producing added cuts in US readiness and power projection capabilities, rather than alleviating the resource problems in these areas.

The Clinton Administration's FY1997 budget request asks for $242.6 billion in budget authority and $248.2 billion in outlays. These totals are about 6% lower in real terms than the budget level the Congress approved for FY1996. They also include $1.13 billion for a new budgeting category for ongoing peacekeeping operations, which means the money available for past expenditures is smaller than the total implies.

The Clinton Administration's future budget plans show a rise in spending in current dollars that accelerates sharply after FY 2000—the last year of a second Clinton Administration, if the President should be reelected:

- Total defense budget authority in current dollars is planned to increase from an actual spending level of $266.3 billion in FY1995 to $263.3 billion in FY1996, $254.4 billion in FY1997, $258.8 billion in FY1998, $264.1 billion in FY1999, $270.5 billion in FY2000, $279.6 billion in FY2001, and $287.9 billion in FY2002. These authority figures are higher than the figures for the Department of Defense alone, because they include defense-related spending by other agencies like the Department of Energy.[10]
- Total defense budget outlays in current dollars are planned to increase from an actual spending level of $272.1 billion in FY1995 to $265.6 billion in FY1996, $258.7 billion in FY1997, $254.8 in FY1988, $256.5 billion in FY1999, $262.9 billion in FY2000, $266.0 billion in FY2001, and $275.5 billion in FY2002. These outlay figures include the new money to be spent during a given budget year by the Department of Defense and other agencies like the Department of Energy.[11]

These projected rises in current dollars, however, disguise a very different trend in real defense spending. Department of Defense budget authority in constant dollars is projected to decline by a total of 9.3% between FY1994 and FY2001, and total spending in budget outlays is projected to decline by 18.8%.[12] Few budget analysts believe such spending levels can sustain the forces levels called for in the current US force plans, particularly given the fact that outlays (actual spending) are planned to decline at twice the level of authorizations (current and future spending).

A careful examination of the data also reveals that the projected rise in Budget Authority is much more rapid than the rise in Budget Outlays. As a result, the actual increase in annual cash outlays during FY1997–FY2002 is limited. Department of Defense budget authority is supposed to rise by $5.8 billion in FY1998, $6.2 billion in FY1999, $7.4 billion in FY2000, $7.9 billion in FY2001, and $7.0 billion in FY2002. However, budget outlays are projected to drop by $3.6 billion in FY1998, and only increase by $2.6 billion in FY1999. They do not start to rise significantly until FY2000, when they rise by $6.4 billion. They then rise by only $3.7 billion in FY2001, and then jump up $8.3 billion in FY2002.[13]

It is hardly coincidence that this spending pattern seems to promise a major rise in budget authority—the figure normally used by analysts to measure an Administration's commitment to national security—while it minimizes the rise in outlays—the figure that affects the calculations relating to the balancing of the budget. The projected budget allows a second Clinton Administration to seem stronger on defense while deferring the major impact of any rise in actual spending until well after the Administration is over.

In addition, the current FYDP assumes a $17.8 billion savings from base realignments and closings during FY1997–FY2002, but past experience indicates that such base closing activity actually raise defense spending for environmental and political reasons. Similarly, the Department of Defense is counting on up to a $30 billion "windfall" between FY1997 and FY2002, because it now estimates that inflation will be lower than previously expected. As a result, the overall pressures on defense spending could be much greater than anticipated.[14]

Finally, the US has only begun to come to grips with the problem of counterproliferation and to develop the programs it will need. Developing a new strategy, tactics, and forces to deal with weapons of mass destruction is a key priority for defending the Gulf. However, the FYDP currently allocates only limited development funds for such programs. As a result, there is a major aspect of US force requirements that is not even costed, much less included in US spending plans.

The Growing Crisis in Defense Procurement

The net impact of these fiscal problems on US capability to conduct a major campaign in Southwest Asia is clearest in the case of procurement. The Clinton Administration's defense procurement request for the FY1997 budget totaled $39.9 billion. To put this funding level in perspective, procurement spending has declined from $137.5 billion in FY1985 to less than $50 billion in FY1994, or by over 60% between FY1985 and FY1996. Table One shows that procurement spending has declined by 53% since the Gulf War alone.

This decline increased by nearly 10% in FY1997, in spite of pledges a year before to halt the decline beginning with the FY1997 budget submission. In fact, Secretary of Defense William Perry had warned as late as January, 1996, that the US could be forced into significant additional force cuts if Congress did not fund the $50–60 billion in annual weapons modernization for which the FY1997–FY2001 defense program had called. As a result, the FY1997 figure effectively deferred any effort to support the modernization of US forces until FY1998.

The revised projections included with the FY1997 budget submission called for annual real procurement spending to rise to $60.1 billion in FY2002. If this program were actually funded, it would mean a slow rise in annual real procurement spending of 40% by FY2002.[15] However, such funding would fall far short of US requirements even if it is funded. The Joint Staff estimated the cost of US procurement requirements in FY1997 alone at $75 billion. It felt this figure was too "unaffordable" to send to Secretary Perry and the president, but still requested $65 billion. Chairman of the Joint Staff General John Shalikashivili stated in January 1996 that that the procurement budget should be at least $60 billion beginning in FY1998, but the Department of Defense's projected procurement request for FY1998 was only $48.5 billion.[16]

Much of the planned rise in procurement funding during FY1997–FY2002 was also programmed to occur after the end of a second term—if President Clinton were reelected. It seemed to be more of a political effort to defuse campaign charges that US military forces were underfunded than a serious effort at military planning. This kind of annual budgetary delay in badly needed modernization, and unrealistic rise in future spending, also has ominous historical precedents. For more than half a decade after Vietnam, the US issued annual FYDPs that promised increased future spending while actual defense budgets declined. The end result of this "rolling get well" was that US forces became "hollow" in force strength, modernization and readiness.[17]

There are also good reasons to doubt whether the procurement funding projected in the FY1997–FY2002 program would be adequate even if future budgets actually provided it. The Secretary of Defense and Chairman of the Joint Chiefs have to be careful about what they can say in public. The Joint Staff, however, has less reason for such caution in preparing its internal studies, such as the annual Chairman's Program Assessment (CPA) which the Joint Staff prepares in October of each year for the Secretary of Defense as part of the planning of the next year's defense budget. In October 1995, the CPA estimated that the US needed to spend at least $65 billion annually on equipment modernization to meet the requirements set forth in the nation's strategy.

The CPA also warned that the US could not make further cuts in force levels and still meet the objectives set forth in US strategy.[18] This same CPA recommended killing a number of programs advocated by Congress, including the B-2, SR-71, and Hunter UAV and eliminating duplicative theater missile defense programs. It advocated increased spending on a number of areas with direct application to power projection—including medium tactical vehicles, counter-proliferation, the Joint Advanced Strike Technology (JAST) fighter, and more Tomahawk missiles to allow deployment on all US submarines.[19]

Furthermore, there are important indications that inadequate US procurement funding has already mortgaged the capability of US forces:

- The US Army estimates that its current modernization budget is only two-thirds of the $15 billion a year it needs to maintain and modernize the equipment in its planned force structure.[20] The estimated scale of the shortfalls in the other three services is similar.
- Tank production has been cut from 720 per year in 1990 to zero (100 tanks are being modernized), ships have been cut from 29 to 7, and aircraft from 943 to 106.[21] As a result, the mid-point system operating life of US tanks and aircraft will have to double between FY1990 and FY1999.
- The Navy has been able to keep its force from aging by retiring nearly 24 combat ships per year. As a result, the average age of the fleet dropped from 15 years in FY1990 to around 10 years in FY1994, and will be less than 13 years in FY2000—well below the desired mid-point system operating life of 18 years. At the same time, ship building funding is not adequate to maintain the fleet in the future. The Navy needs to build 10 to 11 ships a year to stabilize the age of the fleet once current force cuts are completed, but shipbuilding funds dropped to only $75.7 billion in FY1997 and current Navy plans call for building 4 to 7 ships per year.
- Even if all current budget plans are met, equipment in the other services will age much more rapidly. The average age of US Army tanks rose from four years in FY1990 to seven years in FY1994 and is predicted to be 14 years in FY2000; this is one year older than the desired mid-point system operating life of 13 years. The average age of US Air Force fighter and attack aircraft rose from seven years to in FY1990 to eight years in FY1994, but will be 14 years in FY2000, also one year older than the desired mid-point system operating life of 13 years. The average age of US Navy and Marine Corps fighter and attack aircraft only rose from 8 years to in FY1990 to 9 years in FY1994, but it will be 11 years in FY2000—two years younger than the desired mid-point system operating life of 13 years, but far older than at the time of the Gulf War.[22]

Cuts in procurement funds have scarcely stopped all US force improvements. The US is still buying major new programs like the M-1A2 tank upgrade, the DDG-51 destroyer, the F/A-18E/F fighter, a new attack submarine, the V-22 tiltrotor aircraft, the F-22 air superiority fighter, and C-17 strategic transport. It issued a development contract for the JAST fighter in January, 1996—with a potential buy of 1,800 aircraft for the Air Force, 300 for the Navy, and 600 for the Marine Corps in the period after 2005.[23]

However, the US ended a wide range of other force improvement programs. It has eliminated or delayed much of the US Army armor modernization plan. The Navy has terminated the AFX fighter, the EA-6B remanufacture program, CH-53 procurement, and the SH-60B, SH-60F, and HH-60H helicopter programs. It has also had to cut back on mine warfare modernization programs. The Air Force has terminated the Tri-Service Stand-off Attack Missile, F-16 procurement, and procurement of an advanced multi-role attack fighter.

Recent defense budgets and Congressional mark-ups also indicate that cuts and slippages are occurring in procuring such important force improvements as:

- Precision strike capabilities for the F-22, B-1, and B-2;
- The F-22 air defense fighter for the Air Force at the initially planned scale and rate, and providing the F-22 with "stealth" attack capabilities;
- A Joint Advanced Strike Technology next generation aircraft for the Air Force, Navy, and Marine Corps;
- Additional Army prepositioned equipment for heavy armored divisions in Southwest Asia;
- A new generation of more advanced battlefield surveillance, command, control, and communications systems;
- Improved anti-armor systems and ordnance, including all-weather anti-armor submunitions for air delivery, and other new "smart" and "brilliant" munitions;
- Adequate stocks of the Tomahawk missile. The US Navy originally planned to procure 217 Block III missiles per year during 1996–1998. The US now seems likely to fund only 164 missiles in 1996, 120 in 1997, and 100 in 1998. It is unclear such numbers will be adequate. The US fired over 300 missiles during the Gulf War. It fired nearly 70 in two attacks in 1993 designed to force Saddam Hussein to comply with the UN cease-fire accords, and 13 in an attack on Bosnian communications in September, 1995. US doctrine calls for steadily greater use of cruise missiles, and current orders will not allow the Navy to properly arm its submarines and the

number of new ships being equipped with the Vertical Launch System (VLS);[24]

- Additional Army firepower in the form of ATACMS and the multiple launch rocket system (MLRS);
- Firepower for US light divisions. The US Army armored gun system was canceled in 1995, and the program had called for the procurement of 500 advanced artillery weapons;
- Enhanced readiness of Army National Guard combat brigades so that they can deploy in 90, rather than 180 days;
- Equipment and sustainability improvements to keep all three full time active Marine Expeditionary Forces (MEFs)—which are division sized land-air amphibious strike forces—combat ready;
- Improved mine counter-measure and missile defense capabilities; and,[25]
- Providing additional strategic airlift, including the C-17 or a similar capability. The US also has no stable plans to deploy the V-22, new theater missile defenses, or new targeting and attack systems to find and kill mobile missiles and missile launchers.[26]

The key question is what the Congress will do, if anything, to offset these trends. The Congressional mark-up of the Clinton Administration's FY1997 budget request has examined plans to add $13 billion to the Pentagon's modernization efforts. Roughly $2 billion of this total, however, is planned to go to ballistic missile defenses. The Army, Navy, and Air Force would get $3 billion each, and the Marine Corps would get $2 billion. Much of the total would go to development, rather than procurement, and much of the rest would go to areas of interest to given members of Congress—largely in the former of added procurement of combat aircraft—rather than high priority power projection needs.[27]

The Problem of Readiness

There are many similar uncertainties about the levels of readiness the US can maintain with its projected FY1997–FY2002 defense budgets.[28] The chiefs of the US military services testified in their presentations of the FY1997 budget request that readiness is deteriorating, but will not reach the crisis point if planned funding levels are provided, if readiness funds are not diverted to peace making and other missions, and if suitable trade-offs are made to cut expenditures in low-priority areas like surplus infrastructure and facilities.

However, they had given similar testimony each year since FY1993, and readiness funding continued to drop in important areas like major and depot maintenance, stocks of spare parts, munitions stocks, training and education funds, and a host of other areas. The defense budget statements issued after the FY1993 budget stressed that few or no cuts were being made in the operational tempo (Optempo) of military activity, but this reporting disguised the fact that Optempo is only one very general measure of military capability and can disguise a host of smaller cuts in readiness.

There have also been more visible indications of readiness problems. The Navy has only been able to deploy two of the three carrier task forces necessary to maintain its desired maritime presence. Budget cuts have adversely affected the availability of naval air assets, forcing the Navy to address an FY1998 shortfall of six F/A-18 squadrons, the equivalent of 20% of its F/A-18 force. The Navy sought additional funds to correct this shortfall in the FY1997 and FY1998 Program Objective Memorandum (POM), but it is not clear whether they will be provided.

The Army may have to cut its manpower goals by another 20,000 personnel in FY1998 in order to transfer a $1 billion saving to its underfunded modernization program. Even before these cuts, the Army's force structure was so undermanned that it had to consider stripping its eight National Guard divisions of some of their support capabilities so its manpower could be used to augment the Army's current shortfall in non-divisional support assets.[29]

The Chairman of the Joint Chiefs of Staff testified in early 1995, that seven critical enhancements were needed in US forces and capabilities to execute US capability to fight in a major regional contingency. These enhancements included: (1) additional Army prepositioned equipment, (2) additional airlift and sealift, (3) improved anti-armor and precision-guided munitions, (4) more early-arriving naval air, (5) improved Army National Guard combat brigade readiness, (6) improved Army National Guard and reserve support readiness, and (7) improved command, control, communications, and intelligence assets.[30]

Overall Resource Problems and Contingency Capabilities

These basic resource problems inevitably affect US war-fighting capabilities in Southwest Asia. They lead to reductions in sustainability, in key areas of modernization, and in the overall technological "edge" the US once planned to maintain over potential threats in the region. Their cumulative impact has already led some senior US military officers to warn that underfunding could significantly increase US casualties in a major conflict in Southwest Asia.[31]

The military services have also encountered serious problems in adjusting their budgets to preserve readiness and modernization. They have sought to compensate for budget cuts making trade-offs to cut lower priority modernization programs and infrastructure to fund high-priority programs. The Clinton Administration and the Congress, however, have blocked efforts to eliminate unnecessary bases and infrastructure, and the Congress has diverted money to many of the areas the military services have attempted to cut.

The Congress, for example, shifted billions of dollars worth of funding to unrequested military construction programs and reserve and National Guard forces that have no contingency value in most major regional contingencies and would take at least six months to give minimal readiness in high-priority war-fighting roles. This combination of political cowardice in cutting "pork" and politically sensitive programs, and deliberate waste on low or no-priority forces and programs, has already created problems in maintaining force size and sustaining key modernization efforts like the JAST and the US Army's "Force XXI."

At the same time, the US has succeeded in making many important trade-offs as it has down-sized its forces, it has funded many force improvements despite the cuts in defense spending, it has been able to react to many of the lessons of the Gulf War, and it has received growing support from its allies in the region. US contingency capabilities must also be analyzed in terms of the changes the US is making in its strategy, the specific issues affecting US contingency capabilities in the Gulf, and the changing role of friendly and allied forces.

3

The Impact of Strategy: "Base Force" and "Bottom Up Review"

The shifts that the US has made in its strategy and force plans have also had an important impact on US contingency capabilities. They too reflect the impact of fundamental changes in East-West relations, and of the end of the Cold War, the collapse of the Soviet Union, and the Warsaw Pact. They also reflect the impact of major breakthroughs in arms control, such as the INF Treaty and START. As a result, the US has been able to change the focus of its military strategy and force plans to concentrate largely on regional contingencies.

The First Post–Cold War Force Plan: The Bush Administration "Base Force"

These changes in strategy and force plans began during the late 1980s. President Reagan and President Bush signed several of the most sweeping arms control agreements in history. These agreements ended Warsaw Pact superiority in conventional forces, eliminated the deployment of most theater nuclear weapons, and put the US on a path that would reduce the strategic nuclear threat to the United States from more than 20,000 weapons to 3,000.

By 1990, these trends had reached the point where a comprehensive review of US strategy and forces was inevitable, and led the Bush Administration to develop the "Base Force" plan. This plan was developed in late 1989 and the spring of 1990 under the leadership of Secretary of Defense Richard Cheney and Chairman of the Joint Chiefs General Colin Powell, and was announced on August 1, 1990. It reflected the Bush Administration's effort to define both the changes the US should make in its forces during the period from 1990–1997, and to establish a floor under the cuts the Congress would make in defense spending.

The Base Force plan did not attempt to set new US force levels on the basis of specific contingency requirements, but rather represented an estimate of the overall level of down-sizing which was safe given the end of the Cold War. The impact of the new Base Force plan on total US force levels is summarized in Table Two, and it is clear that the Base Force called for the US to reduce defense spending by approximately 20% by FY1995, and to reduce its force levels by 20–25%.

In practice, the Base Force meant reducing US military manpower by 360,000 people between 1991 and 1997, or from 2.0 million to 1.64 million. It called for Army divisions to be cut from 26 to 18 divisions, aircraft carriers from 15 to 12, combat ships from 536 to 448, Air Force fighter wings from 34 to 26, and strategic bombers from 228 to 181. The Base Force plan also called for defense spending to drop to only about 18% of federal spending by FY1997, and to only 3.6% of the GNP.[32]

Ironically, Saddam Hussein invaded Kuwait on virtually the same day the Base Force was made public—immediately changing some of the assumptions on which it was based. Equally important, the accelerating break up of the Soviet Union and Warsaw Pact indicated that the US could make further changes in its strategic priorities. It allowed the US to look beyond the assumptions in the Base Force and shift US planning from a focus on the remaining risks posed by the East, and uncertainties in the East-West arms control process, to a focus on the threats in other regions. It led to fundamental changes in the need for US forces for Europe, naval forces for a blue water conflict with the USSR, and theater and strategic nuclear forces. Further, a growing recession increased the pressure on the Congress to cut defense to fund domestic spending.

The Impact of the First Clinton Administration Budget Plan

The 1992 Presidential campaign did not involve a serious debate over defense, and certainly did not involve any debate over US strategy regarding the Gulf. The Bush campaign defended the Base Force levels, and occasionally criticized the Clinton campaign for being soft on defense. The Clinton campaign said little about defense, except to call for additional funding for defense conversion and for undefined additional cuts in defense spending of $2 billion in 1993, $8.5 billion in 1994, $10.5 billion in 1995, and $16.5 billion in 1996. Clinton called for these defense cuts as part of much larger cuts in total federal spending, and Clinton's campaign literature presented them in terms of political rhetoric. Defense was little more than a passing thought in a campaign that focused almost exclusively on domestic issues.[33]

Clinton's budget cuts proved to be more than campaign rhetoric, however, once the new president came to office. During 1992, an ongo-

TABLE TWO   Comparing the Bush Base Force and the Original Clinton Force Plans

	1985 Actual	1990 Actual	1993 Actual	Bush Plan for 1997	Clinton Plan for 1998/1999
Active military manpower (millions)	2.2	2.1	1.8	1.4–1.64?	1.418
Army active divisions	18	18	14	12	10
Active Navy aircraft carriers	13	15	12	12	11+1
SSNs	100	93	87	80	55?
SSBNS	37	33	22	18	18
Navy ships	545	540	443	432	346
Marine Expeditionary Forces	3	3	3	3	3
Marine Reserve Divisions	1	1	1	1	1
Marine End Strength (1,000s)	198	197	182	—	174
Air Force active fighter wings	—	24	16	15.25	13
Air Force reserve fighter wings	—	12	12	11	7
Total bombers	—	268	201	211	100–184?

Source: Annual reports of the Secretary of Defense, and Base Force and Bottom Up Review briefings to the Senate Armed Services Committee by the Secretary of Defense and Chairman of the Joint Chiefs of Staff.

ing recession had become the dominant political theme that had led to Clinton's victory, and he began his term in office by focusing on economic stimulus and the budget deficit. On February 17, 1993, President Clinton advanced a major new federal spending program for the budget years of FY1994–FY1998, titled a "A Vision for Change in America." This document, and the supporting documentation from the Office of Management for the Budget (OMB), called for major new cuts in defense.[34]

This documentation also showed that the only net cuts were to be in defense spending. While the Clinton plan cut some existing domestic programs, the cuts in these programs were offset by proposals for new expenditures. As a result net non-defense spending actually increased, and defense was taxed in the effort to reduce a budget deficit it had done little to create.[35]

These cuts meant that the force levels in the Base Force were no longer affordable. In the OMB data issued with a "Vision for America," the Administration called for 1998 defense expenditures of $254.2 billion in budget authority in current dollars. This total was 14% less than the $293.4 billion recommended by President Bush, and the Senate Budget Committee staff and the Congressional Budget Office estimate that it was equal to only $232 billion in constant 1994 dollars.[36]

As a result, the Clinton Administration was forced to plan for significant force cuts in the FY1994 budget—long before it could begin to plan such cuts as part of a new strategy. The revised FY1994 budget reduced Navy battle force ships from 443 to 412, and carriers to 12; army active divisions from 14 to 12, and Air Force fighter wings from 28 to 24. The Army was to lose 35,000 personnel, the Navy 46,000, the Marine Corps 8,000, and the Air Force some 19,000. This meant a total cut in US active forces of 108,000 men and women. The plan called for cuts of 60,000 men and women in the Selected Reserves, and 45,000 defense civilians.[37] In addition, the new budget cut procurement spending by 17%. The new budget preserved current levels of operational activity, but other aspects of readiness—such as war reserves, major spares, and depot level maintenance—suffered important cuts.[38]

The Bottom Up Review Process:
"Bottom Up" Versus "Top Down"

This historical background clearly shows that the new strategy the Clinton Administration then developed was not requirements driven. In fact, the new President had already set annual ceilings on defense expenditures for each year through 1998 before such defense planning even began. This meant that strategic planners actually had to work "top down" from a fixed set of fiscal constraints rather than from the "bottom up."

President Clinton left the resulting effort to define a longer term defense program—and the details of his alternative to the Bush Base Force—to his new Secretary of Defense Les Aspin. In March, Aspin announced what he called a "Bottom Up Review" (BUR) of US strategic force plans. He stated that this review was to shape decisions for the FY1995 defense budget and the FY1995–FY1999 Future Years Defense Plan (FYDP). This review was timed to coincide with a broader review of "National Security Strategy and the Role of US Military Forces in the Post–Cold War Era," which was being conducted by the National Security Council as the result of Presidential Review Directive 20.

The tasking for the Bottom Up Review was divided into four main parts. Three of the parts—acquisition programs (with an emphasis on seven major and high cost military systems), selected policy issues, and military service infrastructure—were placed under a Steering Committee chaired by the Under Secretary for Acquisition. The seven key acquisition programs were strategic defense initiative/ballistic missile defense, tactical aircraft, attack submarines, army attack helicopters, space vehicle launchers, military satellite communications, and strategic lift.

The fourth area for review was force structure. This was the responsibility of the Assistant Secretary for Policy, although most of the work on requirements and force structure was actually done by the Office of the Joint Chiefs of Staff and military services. Separate task forces were formed that reported to the Steering Committee. They examined a number of special issues like attack submarines, environmental problems, and acquisition.

All of this effort, however, was conducted to meet the "top down" funding limits already established by the President. In fact, the "top down" character of the Bottom Up Review was reinforced by the fact that its initial recommendations regarding force levels had to be cut still further because of a drop in projected funds.

On March 27, 1993, the new fiscal targets for defense spending directed by the Office of Management and the Budget (OMB) forced Secretary Aspin to submit a revised FY1994 defense budget submission that cut the Bush request for FY1994 by $10.8 billion—to a new total of $266.1 billion. Secretary Aspin then had to cut another $5 billion for each service from the FY1994 budget in early June when unanticipated outlays brought spending above the cap the Congress had set on FY1994 spending. Each of these cuts inevitably reduced the overall spending targets used for planning the new strategy.

The impact of such budget constraints on the recommendations of the Bottom Up Review is illustrated in Table Three, which compares the force

TABLE THREE   Recommended US Force Levels in 1998/99 to "Win in 2 Nearly
Simultaneous Major Regional Conflicts"

Force Requirement	May 8, 1993	September 7, 1993
Active Army divisions	12	10
Army Reserve Units	8 Divisions	15 Enhanced Brigades
Carrier battle groups	12	11+1
Marine Expeditionary Forces (MEFs)	3	3
Marine Reserve Divisions	1	1
Active Fighter Wings	14	13
Reserve Fighter Wings	10	7

Source: Washington Times, September 3, 1993, p. A-8 and Office of the Joint Chiefs of Staff.

levels recommended in May 1993 with those that were finally accepted in September. In effect, the recommended force levels were tailored to the changing estimates of what was affordable, rather than planned from the "bottom up."

Planning for the Bottom Up Review was also complicated by serious problems in virtually every aspect of the planning, management, and budgeting systems of the Department of Defense (DoD). The Department's programming and costing systems proved to be weak, and the Department's long-term cost estimating methods suffered from severe undercosting problems that could not be corrected during the time the Bottom Up Review was in progress. The Department was also poorly prepared to examine many of the problems in regional warfare. US war-gaming and modeling efforts lent themselves far more to Cold War scenarios than the new realities of dealing with major regional conflicts. The Department of Defense has since made major efforts to improve its programming, budgeting, and cost models, but experts from the Comptroller's office still admitted in 1996 that they had major problems in projecting the true outyear costs of the Department's FY1997–FY2002 force plans.

The Detailed Results of the Bottom Up Review

Given this background, it is not surprising that the resulting debates over how best to fit requirements to resources delayed the completion of the Bottom Up Review for several months. This delay, in turn, had a major impact on the ability to transform the result into budget plans. The final results of the Bottom Up Review were only announced on September 1, 1993—after Congress had virtually completed action on the FY1994 defense budget, and so late in the FY1995 defense budget cycle that it became difficult for the US military services to fully revise their defense programs. In a number of cases, planning guidance could not be provided until FY1996. When these results became public, however, the resulting briefings did contain a great deal of detail on the Clinton Administration's proposed strategy and force plans.

The content of the briefing aids the Department of Defense used to describe the results of the Bottom Up Review is summarized in Table Four. It is clear from this table that the new strategy it recommended differed sharply from that of the Base Force to the extent that the Bottom Up Review focused on specific contingency requirements and new priorities like counter-proliferation, rather than down-sizing US forces to reflect the end of the Cold War.

At the same time, the proposed new strategy, deployments, and proposed force requirements were all a natural evolution of US strategy. There were no radical departures from the Bush Base Force, or even from earlier US strategy. The Bottom Up Review preserved the same basic overseas deployments and naval presence that the US has maintained since the 1950, although it places more emphasis on the Gulf and Asia rather than Europe. It calls for cooperative defense, but it preserves US freedom of action and the ability to fight alone.

TABLE FOUR   Details of the Outcome of the Clinton/Aspin Bottom Up Review
            (BUR)

Uses of US Military Forces

- The Bottom Up Review (BUR) develops four broad categories where US military forces can be used:
  - "Dangers posed by nuclear weapons & other weapons of mass destruction, including dangers associated with the proliferation of nuclear, biological, & chemical weapons."
  - "Regional dangers, posed primarily by the threat of large-scale aggression by major regional powers with interests antithetical to our own, but also by the potential for smaller, often internal, conflicts based on ethnic, or religious animosities, state-sponsored terrorism, and subversion of friendly governments."
  - "Dangers to democracy & reform, in the former Soviet Union, Eastern Europe, and elsewhere."
  - "Economic dangers to our national security, which could result if we fail to build a strong, competitive and growing economy."

Major Regional Contingencies

- The most critical aspect of US force planning is the ability to fight two major regional conflicts (MRCs) near simultaneously:
  - The United States does not have to plan to fight a major conflict with Russia.
  - The United States does have to plan to deal nearly simultaneously with a major threat like North Korea and a Gulf nation like Iran and Iraq.
  - Planning for only one major regional conflict would leave the US vulnerable to a threat in another part of the world. Planning to fight such conflicts in sequence would allow the second aggressor to firmly establish itself in defensive positions and greatly increase the forces the US would need to win and the cost of a US victory.
  - North Korea and the Gulf are the most likely major regional conflicts, but the US cannot rely on the ability to predict where it will have to fight.
  - The US must plan to meet potential regional aggressors capable of fielding forces of 400,000–700,000 men, 2,000–4,000 tanks, 3,000–5,000 armored fighting vehicles, 2,000–3,000 artillery pieces, 500–1,000 combat aircraft, 100–200 naval vessels (primarily patrol craft armed with surface to surface missiles) and up to 50 submarines, and 100–1,000 Scud class missiles (possibly armed with nuclear chemical, and/or biological warheads).
  - The US will seek to fight any such conflict as part of a cooperative effort with its allies, the UN, and/or other friendly states.
  - The US must prepare for four phases of conflict: (1) Halt the invasion, (2) build-up US combat power in the theater while reducing the enemy's, (3) decisively defeat the enemy, and (4) provide for post-war stability.

(continues)

TABLE FOUR *(continued)*

- To execute this strategy, the US must improve its strategic airlift, provide rapid sealift for heavy ground and air forces, and preposition heavy combat equipment on land and afloat. It must improve its battlefield surveillance, command, control, and communications capabilities with advanced systems like the MILSTAR satellite, an improved AWACS, and JSTARS. It must also acquire a large number of more advanced "smart" and "brilliant" munitions, and maintain large aerial refueling capabilities.
- The basic building block or force structure necessary to execute the strategy for a single Major Regional Contingency (MRC) is:
    - 4–5 Army divisions
    - 4–5 Marine Expeditionary Brigades
    - 10 Air Force fighter wings
    - 100 Air Force heavy bombers
    - 4–5 Navy aircraft carrier battle groups
    - Special Operations forces
- The force requirements to execute a two nearly simultaneous major regional conflicts is twice the requirement for one major regional conflict.
- Additional forces may be needed for any one major regional conflict, including at least two additional US Army divisions.

Major Force Enhancements

- Developing an adequate capability to fight two nearly simultaneous major regional contingencies (MRCs) requires the US to make major enhancements in its forces.
- *Strategic Mobility*
    - Continue to purchase C-17s
    - Keep an Army brigade set of heavy armor afloat on ships
    - Increase capacity of surge sealift by purchasing additional roll on-roll off (RO-RO) ships
    - Improve readiness and responsiveness of Ready Reserve Force (RRF) ships
    - Fund additional measures to improve fort-to-port flow of personnel, equipment, and supplies
- *Naval Strike Aircraft*
    - Fund a precision ground-attack capability for F-14s
    - Navy will develop a plan to surge additional F/A-18s to forward-deployed aircraft carriers that would be the first to arrive in response to a regional contingency—goal is to increase the strike power of the CVN's
- *Army Firepower*
    - Continue to purchase the Apache Longbow, which will increase the effectiveness and survivability of the AH-64 Apache attack helicopter, and give it a fire and forget capability against armor.
    - Develop new smart submunitions that can be delivered by ATACMS, the Multiple-Launch Rocket System (MLRS), the Tri-Service Stand off Attack Missile (TSSAM), & by standard tube artillery

---

(continues)

TABLE FOUR   (*continued*)

- • Preposition ATACMS, MLRS, and Apaches so they can self-deploy from their overseas bases for quick response
- • *Reserve Component Forces*
  - • Change role of combat Army National Guard units to be prepared to deter or fight a second major regional conflict while the actives are engaged in first major regional conflict
  - • Increase the capability and effectiveness of its Navy/Marine Corps Reserve Air Wing through the introduction of a reserve/training aircraft carrier.

Peace Enforcement and Intervention Operations

- • The US must also plan for peace enforcement and intervention.
- • Typical operations include:
  - • Forced entry into defended airfields, ports, and other facilities and seizing and holding these facilities;
  - • Controlling the movement of troops and supplies across borders and within a target country and enforcing a blockade or quarantine of maritime commerce;
  - • Establishing and defending zones in which civilians are protected from external attacks;
  - • Securing protected areas from internal threats such as snipers, terrorist attacks, and sabotage;
  - • And turning over responsibility for security to peacekeeping units and/or a reconstituted administrative authority.
- • The BUR recommends the following force structure to execute the strategy for a major intervention or peace enforcement operation:
  - • 1 air assault or airborne division
  - • 1 light infantry division
  - • 1 Marine Expeditionary Brigade
  - • 1–2 carrier battle groups
  - • 1–2 composite wings of Air Force aircraft
  - • Special Operations Forces
  - • Civil affairs units
  - • Airlift and sealift force
  - • Combat support and service support units
  - • 50,000 total combat and support personnel
- • These capabilities for peace enforcement will be provided largely by the same collection of general purpose forces needed for the single major regional conflict—so long as those forces had the appropriate training needed for peace-keeping or peace enforcement.

Future US Military Presence Overseas

- • *In Europe*
  - • US will continue to provide leadership in a reinvigorated NATO.
  - • Maintain about 100,000 troops in Europe.

(*continues*)

TABLE FOUR *(continued)*

- Maintain 2 1/3 wings of Air Force fighters in Europe.
- Maintain substantial elements of 2 Army divisions, along with corps head-quarters and other supporting elements. Equipment to bring these in-place divisions to full strength will remain prepositioned in Europe, along with the equipment of one additional division that would deploy to the region in the event of a conflict.
- US Army forces will participate in two multi-national corps with German forces. Their training will focus on rapid deployments to conflicts outside of Europe and non-traditional operations such as peace enforcement, in addition to the long-standing mission of stabilization of central Europe. Their equipment and configuration may change over time.
- US Air Force will continue to provide unique theater intelligence, lift, and all-weather precision strike capabilities.
- US Navy will continue to patrol the Mediterranean Sea and other waters surrounding Europe.
- *In Northeast Asia*
  - Maintain close to 100,000 troops.
  - Commitment to South Korea's security undiminished.
  - Maintain 1 wing of Air Force fighters in Korea.
  - Keep one two-brigade division in South Korea, with prepositioned equipment for third brigade, but eventually redeploy 1 of 2 Army brigades out of South Korea.
  - Maintain 1 Marine Expeditionary Force (MEF) with brigade-sized amphibious force and Marine Air Wing in Okinawa.
  - Maintain 1 Army Special Forces battalion in Okinawa.
  - Continue to home port carrier Independence, amphibious assault ship Bellau Wood, and supporting ships in Japan.
  - Maintain 1 1/2 wings of Air Force fighters in Japan and Okinawa.
  - Preposition one added brigade set ashore in Korea, if the US chooses to withdraw one brigade from the division currently in Korea, and add one prepositioned brigade set afloat that can "swing" between Asia and the Gulf.
  - US 7th Fleet to routinely patrol West Pacific.
  - Increase early-arriving land-based and carrier aircraft and long-range bombers.
  - Enhance air, land, and sea anti-armor capability.
  - Improve anti-tactical ballistic missile capability.
  - Upgrade airlift and sealift to support rapid closure of heavy forces.
- *In SW Asia and the Gulf*
  - Local sensitivities to a large-scale Western military presence require heavier reliance on periodic deployment of forces.
  - Maintain a presence of 4–6 Navy combatants in Middle East Force .
  - Maintain maritime prepositioning ship squadron at Diego Garcia with seven ships.
  - Increase level of prepositioned equipment on land from one brigade in Kuwait by adding a brigade set in another country.

(continues)

TABLE FOUR *(continued)*

- Preposition one "swing" brigade set afloat near the Gulf that could also go to Asia or elsewhere in the world.
- Increase early arriving land-based and carrier aircraft, and long-range bombers.
- Enhance air, land, and sea anti-armor capability.
- Improve anti-tactical ballistic missile capability.
- Upgrade airlift and sealift to support rapid closure of heavy forces.

Future US Naval Presence

- The flexibility of aircraft carriers to operate effectively with relative independence from shore bases, makes them well suited to overseas presence operations especially where land-based military infrastructure is relatively underdeveloped.
- Because of this, the strategy has set ship force structure levels at levels higher than those needed to fight two major regional conflicts. However, the Clinton/Aspin plan is willing to limit the carrier battle groups to 11 active and 1 reserve unit, and gap the presence of carriers in SW Asia, NE Asia, and the Mediterranean for Navy personnel reasons.
- The US will make up for gaps in carrier coverage without a degradation of US maritime presence by deploying:
  - Large deck amphibious assault ship with AV-8B Harriers and Cobra attack helicopters and 2,000 man Marine Expeditionary Brigade
  - Tomahawk sea launched cruise missile-equipped Aegis cruiser/destroyer, a guided missile destroyer, attack subs, and P-3 land-based maritime patrol aircraft
  - Implement strategy of "Adaptive Joint Force Packages" in maritime deployments
- *Strategic Nuclear Forces*
- Changing strategic environment makes it impossible to set firm requirements.
- Cannot ignore threat posed by instability in former Soviet Union.
- Many obstacles must be overcome before ratification of START II, and Ukrainian ratification of START I, and full reductions will not be implemented for 10 years.
- US must maintain significant strategic forces.
  - 18 Trident subs with C-4 & D-5 missiles
  - 500 Minuteman II missiles, each carrying a single warhead
  - 94 B-52H bombers equipped with air launched cruise missiles
  - 20 B-2 bombers

Total US Force Requirements

- *In Army*
  - 10 divisions (active)
  - 5+ divisions (reserve)

(continues)

TABLE FOUR   (*continued*)

- *In Navy*
  - 11 aircraft carriers (active)
  - 1 aircraft carrier (reserve)
  - 45–55 attack subs
  - 346 ships
- *In Air Force*
  - 13 fighter wings (active)
  - 7 fighter wings (reserve)
  - Up to 184 bombers*
- *In Marine Corps*
  - 3 Marine Expeditionary Forces
  - 174,000 personnel end strength (active)
  - 42,000 personnel end strength (reserve)
  - Develop the V-22 Osprey hybrid transport plane
- *In Strategic Nuclear Forces*
  - 18 ballistic missile subs
  - Up to 94 B-52 bombers
  - 20 B-2 bombers*
  - 500 Minuteman III ICBMs (single RV)

Decisions on Core Procurement Programs

- *Theater Missile Defense* (TMD) = $12B for FY1995–99
  - Develop an enhanced version of land-based Patriot
  - Develop Sea-based Aegis/Standard Missile Block IV
  - Develop land-based Theater High-Altitude Area Defense (THAAD)
  - Develop Sea-based Upper Tier System
- *National Missile Defense* (NMD) = $2–3 Billion for FY1995–99
  - Develop Brilliant Eyes
  - Integrate ground-based radar technology wrapped into THAAD
  - Integrate ground based interceptor (GBI) technology into THAAD & Sea-based Upper Tier
- *Theater Air Forces*
  - Proceed with the development & procurement of F/A-18EF
  - Retire all A-6 aircraft by 1998 (before production of EF)
  - Proceed with the development & procurement of F-22 (incorporate a limited air-to-ground capability from outset)
  - Cancel the A/F-X and MRF, and F-16 production after FY1994
  - Launch a Joint Advanced Strike Technology Program
- *Aircraft Carriers*
  - Proceed with construction of CVN-76 beginning in FY1995
  - Delay advance procurement for CVN-77 until after FY1999
  - Maintain a naval force structure built around 11 active aircraft carriers, 10 Navy active air wings, and one composite Navy-Marine Corps reserve air wing.

(*continues*)

TABLE FOUR   (*continued*)

- Proceed to establish a reserve/training carrier to provide Navy and Marine pilots their initial carrier training, to train Navy & Marine Reserve pilots, and for occasional forward deployments, to give more realistic training to reserve air crews while filling gaps in overseas presence.
- *Attack Submarines*
  - Maintain a force of 45–55 attack subs
  - Produce a second and third Seawolf attack sub & direct production to Groton, Connecticut, shipyard to try to bridge the projected gap in sub production & mitigate the risk to the industrial base. (This decision does not allow Tenneco, Newport News shipyard to compete for SSN-23).

Note: "Totals differed according to date of briefing charts. Some charts only refer to "up to 100 bombers."

Source: Based on a combination of the tables and text provided by Secretary of Defense Aspin to the House and Senate Armed Services Committees while presenting the results of the Bottom Up Review in September 1993. Although dated September 1, 1993, several tables were revised, added, or deleted during September 1st through September 14th.

4

The Focus of US Planning and Strategy Shifts to Major Regional Contingencies

Many of the details regarding the nature of US planning for a major regional conflict in the Gulf remain classified. It is clear, however, that Secretary Aspin took a decision early in the Bottom Up Review process to choose force packages associated with a strategy and force requirements that called for an American capability to win two nearly simultaneous major regional conflicts. In the briefing materials Aspin released on September 1, 1993, he justified this decision by stating: [39]

> This is prudent for two reasons: First, we need to avoid a situation in which the United States in effect makes simultaneous wars more likely by leaving an opening for potential aggressors to attack their neighbors, should our engagement in a war in one region leave little or no force available to respond effectively to defend our interests in another.
>
> Second, fielding forces sufficient to win two wars nearly simultaneously provides a hedge against the possibility that a future adversary—or coalition of adversaries—might one day confront us with a larger-than expected threat. In short, it is difficult to predict precisely what threats we will confront ten to twenty years from now. In this dynamic and unpredictable post–Cold War world, we must maintain military capabilities that are flexible and sufficient to cope with unforeseen threats.
>
> For the bulk of our ground, naval and air forces, fielding forces sufficient to provide this capability involves duplicating the major regional contingency (MRC) building block described above. However, in planning our overall force structure, we must recognize two other factors. First, we must have sufficient strategic lift to deploy forces when and where we need them. Second, certain specialized high-leverage units or unique assets might be "dual tasked," that is used in both major regional conflicts.

Secretary Aspin also stated in a booklet on the Bottom Up Review, released by the Department of Defense on September 1st, that,

Every war the United States has fought has been different from the last, and different from what defense planners had envisioned. For example, the majority of the bases and facilities used by the US and its Coalition partners during Desert Storm were built in the 1980s, when we envisioned a Soviet invasion through Iran to be the principal threat to the Gulf region. In planning forces capable of fighting and winning major regional conflicts, we must avoid preparing for past wars. History suggests that we most often deter the conflicts we plan for and actually fight the ones we do not anticipate.

The Phases of Conflict in the New US Strategy

As part of this shift to a regional strategy, US planners began to come to grips with the fact that the US had to act rapidly and decisively in both the Gulf and Northeast Asia if US forces were to be effective. As a result, they analyzed major regional conflicts in terms of US ability to successfully implement four phases of conflict: (1) halting the invasion; (2) building up US combat power in the theater while reducing the enemy's; (3) decisively defeating the enemy; and (4) providing for postwar stability:

The phases of conflict were defined as follows:[40]

- *In the case of phase one, the "Halt the Invasion" phase,* US planners placed great emphasis on rapidly blunting and halting an enemy invasion, helping allied forces check enemy ground forces, and disrupting and damaging enemy ground forces throughout the attacking country with attacks using missiles and advanced air munitions. The US planned to rapidly enhance air and missile defenses, establish air superiority, provide enhanced reconnaissance and electronic warfare systems, and deploy long-range strike aircraft and surface-to-surface missile systems like the US Army's Army Tactical Missile System (ATACMS). It planned to establish maritime superiority, and rapidly deploy improved mine countermeasure capabilities to secure ports and as a precondition for amphibious assault.
- During this phase, the US planned to conduct the same kind of strategic air and missile offensive it executed during Desert Storm. It planned to suppress enemy air defenses as needed, including those in rear areas and supporting the invading ground forces, and to destroy high value enemy targets such as weapons of mass destruction, central command, control, and communications facilities, and key stockpiles, supplies, and support capabilities. Such an offensive would both deny the enemy the ability to threaten the use of weapons of mass destruction and severely degrade the enemy's ability to conduct combat operations.

- *In phase two, the "Build up US Combat Power in the Theater While Reducing the Enemy's" phase*, the US was supposed to steadily build up its capability for a ground counteroffensive, while adding air and sea-based air and missile forces. It would use these forces to shift from halting the invasion to isolating enemy ground forces and destroying them, destroying enemy air and naval forces, destroying stocks of supplies, and broadening attacks on military related targets in the enemy's rear. At the same time, US heavy ground forces would prepare and move forward for the counteroffensive.
- *In phase three, the "Decisively defeat the enemy" phase*, US planners called for the US and allied forces to seek to mount a large-scale, air-land offensive to defeat the enemy decisively by attacking his center of gravity, retaking occupied territory, destroying his war-making capabilities, and successfully achieving other operational or strategic objectives.
- *Finally, in the "provide for post-war stability phase,"* US planners indicated that the majority of US and coalition forces would be returning to their home bases, but some forces would be called upon to remain in the theater after the enemy had been defeated to ensure the conditions that resulted in conflict did not recur. These forces were supposed to help repatriate prisoners, occupy and administer all or some of the enemy's territory, and/or ensure compliance with the provisions of war-termination or cease-fire agreements.

These four phases have obvious importance in any Gulf conflict. In spite of Aspin's warning, "Every war the United States has fought has been different from the last," these phases were also remarkably similar to the way the US fought Desert Storm. While changing the initial speed of US land and land-based air deployments, and calling for other enhancements to US force capabilities based on the lessons of the Gulf War, in many ways this strategy prepared for the next war by making the US ready to fight the last conflict.

The Nominal Threat and the US Forces Required to Win Two Near Simultaneous Major Regional Conflicts

The briefings on the Bottom Up Review did not discuss regional threats in any detail. The Department of Defense talked in general terms about the forces and force improvements the US would require for a major contingency (4–5 Army divisions, 4–5 Marine Expeditionary Brigades, 10 Air Force fighter wings, 100 Air Force heavy bombers, 4–5 Navy aircraft carrier battle groups, special operations forces). It did not mention the risks involved in committing such force packages to contingencies where an enemy had already gained a significant advantage through surprise, where friendly defenses had begun to collapse, where the US did not have the full support of a major regional ally, and where the attacker initiated biological, chemical, or nuclear warfare at the start of the conflict.[41]

This did not mean, however, that the US failed to plan to meet significant threats in Asia and the Gulf. The nominal threat the US used for planning purposes for each region was obviously sized to include the total forces of major potential threats like Iran and Iraq. The nominal threat included 400,000–700,000 men, 2,000–4,000 tanks, 3,000–5,000 armored fighting vehicles (AFVs) and armored personnel carriers (APCs), 2,000–3,000 artillery pieces, 500–1,000 combat aircraft, 100–200 naval vessels (primarily patrol craft armed with surface-to-surface missiles) and up to 50 submarines, and 100–1,000 Scud class missiles (possibly armed with nuclear, chemical, and/or biological warheads).[42]

It is interesting to compare these US estimates of a nominal threat to the current forces of Iran, Iraq, and North Korea:

- Iran has 465,000–513,000 men, 1,245–1,440 tanks, 970–1,100 armored fighting vehicles and APCs, 2,950 artillery pieces, 295–305 combat aircraft, 54 naval vessels (primarily patrol craft armed with surface-to-surface missiles), two submarines, and 100–300 Scud class missiles (possibly armed with chemical and biological warheads).[43]
- Iraq has 350,000–382,000 men, 2,200–2,700 tanks, 4,400 armored fighting vehicles and APCs, 1,980 artillery pieces, 310–360 combat aircraft, 17 naval vessels (primarily patrol craft armed with surface-to-surface missiles), no submarines, and an unknown number of Scud class missiles with possible chemical, and/or biological warheads.[44]
- North Korea has 1,000,000–1,128,000 men, 3,400 tanks, 2,740 armored fighting vehicles and APCs, 9,700 artillery pieces, 509 combat aircraft, 80 armed helicopters 441 naval vessels (primarily patrol craft armed with surface-to-surface missiles), 25 submarines, and an unknown number of Scud class missiles with chemical, and possible biological warheads.[45]

It is clear from such a comparison that US planners faced a significantly larger threat in an Asian contingency than in the Gulf, unless Iran and Iraq joined forces. As a result, the nominal threat used in the Bottom Up Review represented either the kind of force strengths that Iran and Iraq might develop after the year 2000, or left a significant margin of safety between the nominal threat used for planning and the threat the US actually faced in the Gulf.

The US did not, however, size the recommendations that came out of the Bottom Up Review solely in terms of "worst-case" threats. It also planned its forces for conflicts that emphasized many of the problems the US faced in rapidly deploying combat ready forces from the US to the Gulf. They examined "short notice" enemy attacks involving "armor heavy, combined arms offensives against neighboring states." Such scenarios assumed that the bulk of the US forces involved would not be present in the region when hostilities commenced, would have to deploy quickly, would have to rapidly supplement indigenous forces, halt the invasion, and defeat the aggressor.

Key US Force Improvements

The briefing materials on the Bottom Up Review also called for a long series of changes in US capabilities—almost all of which were designed to improve US power projection and rapid deployment forces in ways that affect future US contingency capabilities in the Gulf.

This list of force improvement requirements is summarized in Table Five, and it is important to note that virtually all of these force improvements have been funded in some form in spite of the cutbacks in US defense spending. The US military services may not have been able to afford all of the force improvements called for in the Bottom Up Review, but they have still been able to improve many of the capabilities of their remaining forces since the Gulf War.[46]

TABLE FIVE   Force Improvements Required in the Bottom Up Review (BUR) Force

- Providing precision strike capabilities for the F-14, F-22, B-1, and B-2.
- Procuring the F-18E/F for the Navy and the F-22 for the Air Force (2003).
- Establishing a Joint Advanced Strike Technology Program for next generation aircraft which mixes new joint munitions, technology demonstrators, and advances in critical components.
- Providing additional Army prepositioned equipment. Improving prepositioning for heavy armored divisions in South Korea and Southwest Asia, and prepositioning one heavy armored brigade set afloat.
- Providing a new generation of far more advanced battlefield surveillance, command, control, and communications systems including JSTARS, an upgraded AWACS, the MILSTAR satellite communications system, new damage assessment and identification of friend and foe systems.
- Providing greatly improved anti-armor systems and ordnance, including all-weather anti-armor submunitions for air delivery, and other new "smart" and "brilliant" munitions.
- Enhancing aerial refueling capabilities to improve power projection capabilities, extend strike and air defense ranges, and increase the tempo and intensity of air operations.
- Buying additional Army firepower in the form of ATACMS, the multiple launch rocket system (MLRS), and the Tri-Service Standoff Attack Missile (TSSAM). Buying the Longbow, fire and forget stand-off anti-tank missile for the AH-64 Apache attack helicopter. Prepositioning more of these systems overseas.
- Enhancing the readiness of Army National Guard combat brigades so they can deploy in 90, rather than 180 days.
- Adding additional Marine Corps end strength, and providing equipment and sustainability improvements to keep all three full time active Marine Expeditionary Forces (MEFs)—which are division sized land-air amphibious strike forces—combat ready.
- Developing and deploying the V-22.
- Compensating for cuts in carrier battle groups, and limitations in future deployment capabilities, by deploying enhanced amphibious assault groups built around large-deck amphibious assault ships with AV-8Bs and Cobra attack helicopters, and a 2,000 man Marine Expeditionary Unit (MEU), or a naval task force built around the Aegis guided-missile cruiser, the Tomahawk sea-launched cruise missile, attack submarines, and land-based P-3 maritime patrol aircraft.
- Improving mine counter-measure and missile defense capabilities.
- Developing the organization, tactics, training, and equipment to deploy "Adaptive Force Packages" that contain joint force packages of air, land, special operations, and maritime forces tailored to meet a theater commander's power projection needs.

(*continues*)

TABLE FIVE   (*continued*)

- Providing additional strategic airlift, including the C-17 or a similar capability, and additional rapid sealift and roll-on roll-off ships. Improving the readiness of the Ready Reserve Force (RRF) for rapid deployment of maritime supply capability, and restructuring basing and infrastructure to improve "fort to port" capabilities.
- Preserving the carrier industrial base.
- Preserving the submarine industrial base.
- Restructuring the Ballistic Missile Defense Program and providing new theater missile defenses. Developing and deploying a mix of improved Patriot PAC-3, THAAD land-based anti-theater ballistic missile, and AEGIS SM-2 Block IVA anti-theater ballistic missile defenses.
- Developing and possibly deploying new targeting and attack systems to find and kill mobile missiles and missile launchers.
- Improving transfer of key weapons and equipment to critical regional allies like South Korea, Saudi Arabia, and Kuwait.

Source: Based on a combination of the tables and text provided by Secretary of Defense Aspin to the House and Senate Armed Services Committees while presenting the results of the Bottom Up Review in September, 1993. Although dated September 1, 1993, several tables were revised, added, or deleted during September 1st through September 14th.

5

US Plans for a Major Regional Contingency in Southwest Asia

The US planners developing contingency plans for Southwest Asia learned two important lessons from the "Tanker War" of 1987–1988, and the Gulf War. They learned that the US could fight effectively in coalitions with Southern Gulf forces, and obtain great benefits from the Southern Gulf states in basing, logistics, support and infrastructure. They also learned that the prepositioning and rapid deployment arrangements the US originally made to deal with the Soviet threat were of equal value in dealing with the threat from Iran and Iraq.

US planners could also take into account the military results of the Iran-Iraq War and Gulf War. They could base their calculations on the fact that Iran had lost nearly 50% of its inventory of major land weapons in its climactic defeats by Iraq in 1988, and had not had major new deliveries of high technology weapons since the fall of the Shah. Further, they could take account of Iraq's massive losses during the Gulf War, and the fact Iraq could not obtain major military resupply until UN sanctions were lifted.

At the same time, the US planners working on Gulf contingencies at the time of the Bottom Up Review felt they were dealing with two hostile regimes whose conduct was unpredictable, which might take actions that could escalate to major conflicts, and which would rebuild their military capabilities as soon as they were given the opportunity to do so. They also felt they had to plan to deal with both current and future Iranian and Iraq capabilities, rather than intentions. As a result, US planners concluded that the only way to deter Iran and Iraq was to maintain a US military presence in the Gulf, develop the ability to rapidly deploy massive amounts of US air power and substantial amounts of US armor, and find ways of strengthening Southern Gulf forces as much as possible.

In the case of Iran, the US saw the primary mid-term threats as an Iranian airborne or amphibious intervention in the case of a revolt or upheaval in a Southern Gulf state, Iranian attempts to become the dominant naval and air power in the Gulf and to use this power to influence oil prices and quotas and political decisions, and Iranian attempts to use growing capabilities to deliver weapons of mass destruction to achieve the same ends. US planners concluded that these threats could be dealt with through naval forces, air forces, and improved missile defenses.

Iraq presented different problems. US planners privately saw no prospect that either Kuwait or any foreseeable combination of Saudi and Kuwait forces could either deter or defend against Iraqi ground forces, or that the Gulf Cooperation Council would produce the kind of unified and effective ground forces that could accomplish such an objective. They estimated that Kuwait City would be particularly vulnerable to a sudden or surprise Iraqi attack, and that all of Kuwait and the Eastern Province of Saudi Arabia would be vulnerable if the US could not provide immediate help. They treated Iraq as a hostile and revanchist state, and concluded that the US had to plan to supplement friendly regional forces with the rapid deployment of US Army and US Marine Corps ground forces.

US planners would have liked to preposition the equipment for two full heavy divisions in Saudi Arabia and Kuwait, and in locations that allowed the US to rapidly airlift in troops and deploy forward to defend the Kuwaiti-Iraqi and Saudi-Iraqi borders. The US had such equipment in the Gulf as a result of the Gulf War, and was disbanding many of the active forces that had used it in the past as a result of the end of the Cold War. The US quickly found, however, that Saudi Arabia would not accept the facilities and manpower necessary to maintain such prepositioned equipment. This meant US planners were forced to rely on much more limited prepositioning in other countries, and on the periodic deployment of US forces in exercises and training activity.[47]

As a result, the Bottom Up Review made much more limited recommendations regarding a forward presence and prepositioning. It called for the US to keep a naval headquarters in Bahrain, and maintain a presence of 4–6 Navy combatant ships in the Middle East Force in the Gulf. It emphasized informal cooperation with Saudi Arabia in maintaining a limited US air presence, and in improving Saudi C^4I/battle management capabilities, making Saudi air and land forces interoperable with US forces, and improving Saudi basing and infrastructure to support both Saudi and US forces in defending Kuwait and meeting other defensive needs in the Gulf.

The Review called for the US to maintain a maritime prepositioning ship squadron at Diego Garcia with seven ships, although it did not support the requirement for an additional ship called for by the Marine Corps. It sought to increase the level of prepositioned US Army equipment in or near the Gulf to a level of three heavy armored brigades. This included prepositioning equipment on land for one brigade in Kuwait, and an additional brigade set in another country. It also included prepositioning of one "swing" brigade set at sea that would normally be deployed afloat near the Gulf, but which could go to Asia or elsewhere in the world. This prepositioning was intended to implement a critical lesson of Desert Storm: the need to have at least one heavy division in place to halt an Iraqi invasion within 7–14 days.

At the same time, the US concluded that there was no practical way to prevent Iraq from rebuilding its offensive armored capabilities at some point in the future, and that the capabilities that had survived the Gulf War already presented a serious threat. At the same time, it concluded that the expansion of Southern Gulf military forces would be too slow and lacking in coordination to provide the kind of quick reaction, rapid maneuver, 24 hour-a-day, war-fighting capability needed to halt Iraq early in an attack and offset Iraq's advantage in numbers. As a result, the Bottom Up Review called for a US capability to deploy a total of at least three heavy divisions within 21–30 days. It also called for the US to provide the required sealift by expanding both the number of roll-on, roll-off ships and the capabilities of its Ready Reserve Force (RRF).

Other recommended force improvements included increasing the number of early arriving US land-based and carrier aircraft, and long-range bombers, and ensuring that these could be supported immediately in high sortie rate attacks on Iranian and Iraqi forces. They included enhancing air, land, and sea anti-armor capability with "smart" or brilliant weapons, and improving targeting and damage assessment capabilities in the region. They included creating an anti-tactical ballistic missile capability that would combine the use of the improved Patriot by Kuwait, Saudi Arabia, and other Southern Gulf countries with advanced US land and sea-based anti-tactical ballistic missile forces. These ballistic missile defenses were to involve dual-capable systems which would also enhance air and cruise missile defense.[48]

Although no specific reference is made to this in the Bottom Up Review, it is clear that these US plans depended on an informal alliance with Saudi Arabia and the other Southern Gulf states for its success. The Bottom Up Review shifted the US force posture in the region from "over-the-horizon" to "low profile" or "off-the-coast," although this shift in strategy still presented the risk that one or more key Gulf countries would react too late, or would give in to Iranian or Iraqi intimidation. This, however, was an unavoidable risk, and one that the level of cooperation between the US and Southern Gulf States during the Iran-Iraq War and Gulf War indicated was acceptable.

Further, US planners concluded that the improvements in US contingency capabilities necessary to deal with the potential threats in Southwest Asia would be adequate to meet any contingency involving Egypt, Israel, or any other regional power, as well as contingencies in the Mediterranean, southern and central Europe, and South Asia.

US Capabilities in Southwest Asia
Since the Bottom Up Review

The years since the Bottom Up Review have led to a number of contradictory trends in US capabilities in Southwest Asia. US planners have been forced to make complex trade-offs, as they attempt to deal with the conflict between the "top down" goals set by the Clinton budget and the "bottom up" force goals established by US defense planners.

These trade-offs do not necessarily reduce US capabilities for a single contingency like the Gulf, but they do mean some reduction in sustainability, in several key areas of modernization, and in the overall technological "edge" that the US had originally planned to maintain over potential threats in the region. The Clinton Administration and the Congress have been confronted by a series of "Hobson's choices." They have had to choose between cutting force strength, readiness, and modernization and so far have compromised by cutting all three.

There is also no question that the US no longer has the same total pool of forces it drew upon during the Gulf War. In early 1996, the US had 27% less active military manpower than at the time of Desert Storm, 30% fewer active Army divisions, 32% fewer battle force ships, and 36% fewer attack and fighter aircraft. At the end of the Clinton planning period, proposed cuts will produce a 45% reduction in active Army divisions relative to Desert Storm, a 50% reduction in reserve component divisions, a 37% reduction in battle force ships, a 27% reduction in carriers, a 23% reduction in active carrier air wings, and a 50% reduction in reserve carrier air wings. There will also produce a 46% cut in active Air Force fighter wings and a 42% cut in reserve wings.

The recent and planned cuts in major US combat units since the Gulf War and Bottom Up Review are shown in Table Six. These cuts, however, are only part of the story. The US has made cuts in its major weapons numbers that are often much more serious than the cuts in major combat unit numbers imply.

In the case of the Army, there will be a 34% cut in tanks, a 41% cut in other active armored fighting vehicles, a 17% cut in major artillery weapons, a 25% cut in surface-to-air missile launch units, a 53% cut in short range air defense systems, and a 31% cut in tactical wheeled vehicles. This latter cut alone raises serious questions about the credibility of a two major regional contingency strategy since the US Army deployed roughly 76% of its inventory of many types of wheeled tactical vehicles during the Gulf War and had large numbers of commercial and Saudi wheeled vehicles as well. The Army will also make a 41% cut in fixed wing aircraft, a 39% cut in active attack helicopters, a 31% cut in active medium lift helicopters, a 100% cut in active heavy lift helicopters, a 30% cut in active utility helicopters. If reserve aircraft are included, the Army will cut its total aircraft strength by 49%.[49]

TABLE SIX   Evolving US Force Plans

Force Element	Gulf War FY1990	Bush Base Force Plan	FY1995	FY1997	Current Clinton Goal for 2002
Army					
Active divisions	18	12	12	10	10
Active Separate Brigades	8	—	3	3	—
Reserve brigades*	57	34	46	46	42
Active personnel (1,000s)	751	—	510	495	475–495
Reserve personnel (1,000s)	736	—	629	603	—
Marines					
Expeditionary Forces**	3	3	3	3	3
Active personnel (1,000s)	197	—	174	174	174
Reserve personnel (1,000s)	45	—	41	42	—
Active Divisions	3	3	3	3	3
Reserve Divisions	1	1	1	1	1
Active Combat Aircraft	368/24	—	332/23	332/23	—
Reserve Combat Aircraft	84/8	—	60/5	48/4	—
Navy					
Active personnel (1,000s)	583	—	439	407	394
Reserve personnel (1,000s)	149	—	101	99	—
Navy Aircraft Carriers	15/1	12/1	11/1	11/1	11/1
Carrier Air Wings	13/2	11/2	10/1	10/1	10/1
Active Combat Aircraft	662/57	—	504/37	420/35	—
Reserve Combat Aircraft	97/9	—	38/3	38/3	—
Battle Force Ships	546	430	373	357	346
Support Forces Ships	66	—	29	25	—

(continues)

TABLE SIX   (continued)

Force Element	Gulf War FY1990	Bush Base Force Plan	FY1995	FY1997	Current Clinton Goal for 2002
Reserve Force Ships	31	—	18	18	—
Ballistic Missile Submarines	34	16	16	17	14
Air Force					
Active personnel (1,000s)	539	—	400	381	375
Reserve personnel (1,000s)	45	—	41	42	—
Fighter Forces					
Active Wing Equivalents	24	15	13	13	13
Active Combat Aircraft	1722/76	—	936/53	900/51	—
Reserve Wing Equivalents	12	11	8	7	7
Reserve Combat Aircraft	873/43	—	567/38	489/38	—
Strategic Bombers***	268	176	141	127	150+
Conventional Bombers	33	—	0	0	—
Strategic Lift					
Intertheater aircraft	400	—	374	376	—
Intratheater aircraft	460	—	416	428	—
Active Sealift Ships					
Tankers	28	—	18	18	—
Cargo	40	—	51	51	—
Reserve Ships	96	—	77	80	—

Notes: *An approximate equivalent and numbers are not comparable in the outyears. The BUR plan calls for 15 enhanced readiness brigades, a goal that DoD will begin to reach in FY1996. Backing up this force will be an Army National Guard strategic reserve of eight divisions (24 brigades), two separate brigade equivalents, and a scout group.

**A MEF includes a Marine division, air wing, and force service support group.

***Numbers differ from the BUR. They only include primary aircraft inventory and exclude aircraft in depot maintenance.

Source: William J. Perry, *Annual Report to the President and the Congress,* Department of Defense, Washington, February 1995, p. 274.

The cuts in US Navy strength are difficult to measure because of the number of different ship types, but the US Navy will have cut 100% of its battleships, about 30% of its active CGs and 78% of its CGNs, 100% of its FFs, and 34% of its FGGs. It will have eliminated 23% of its amphibious ships. It will have cut its active primary combat aircraft by 47%, its active ASW and patrol aircraft by 42%, and its active support aircraft by 42%. The US Marine Corps will have cut its active primary combat aircraft by 17%, and its active electronic warfare, observation, and refueling aircraft by 19%. It will have cut its reserve primary combat aircraft by 50%; its active electronic warfare, observation, and refueling aircraft by 19%; and its total reserve helicopters by 11%.[50]

The US Air Force will have cut its active bomber strength by 44%. It will have cut its active fighter/attack strength by 48% and its reserve strength by 48%. It will have cut the number of its active reconnaissance and special purpose aircraft by 48% and the number of its reserve aircraft by 96%. It will have increased its active special operations aircraft, but largely eliminated its reserve special operations aircraft. It will have reduced its number of active aircraft from 556 to 386, although its reserve aircraft will have increased slightly from 391 to 396. Figures are not available on the goal for tanker forces, but the number of active tankers has already been cut from 533 to 321, while the number of reserve tankers has been increased from 146 to 291.[51]

US Power Projection Capabilities, Strategic Warning, and a "One MRC" Strategy

These changes in the total size of US forces inevitably limit the power the US can project overseas, a critical factor in analyzing US war-fighting capabilities in the Gulf. It is US expeditionary capabilities—not the force totals shown in Table Six—which determine US power projection capabilities.

These US expeditionary capabilities are now limited to the deployment of about one corps of ground troops over a period no shorter than 75 days, plus several additional light US Army divisions and up to two Marine Expeditionary Forces. The US also can only deploy and support about 50–66% of its 13 USAF fighter wings, and 50–66% of its US Navy and Marine Corps tactical air power, in sustained combat.

Put differently, the US can only deploy about 45% to 60% of the total deployable land forces to any one contingency that the US used to create a two Corps force in Desert Storm, and only about 60–70% of the total air power. It is also important to note in this context that the US often employed 60% or more of its world-wide assets of special purpose aircraft and logistic equipment during Desert Storm, and these total assets have since suffered from significant force cuts.[52]

Further, US contingency capabilities depend heavily on strategic warning. The US has many rapid deployment capabilities that can deal with low to mid-intensity conflicts. It takes time, however, to deploy and sustain a full corps of expeditionary forces and the massive levels of air power the US would need for a high-intensity or major regional conflict in the Gulf.

The US needs two to three months of strategic warning, and must fully act on that warning to use its airlift and sealift to fully deploy for one major regional contingency of the size used for planning the Bottom Up Review. It would take additional months to redeploy US forces for a second contingency. Further, the US would begin to encounter major problems from a lack of long lead-spares if it suffered serious attrition in even one contingency and does not have the stocks of munitions and supplies to support two near simultaneous intense conflicts or the industrial base to rapidly replenish its existing stocks. The US would face particular problems in producing the advanced and precision-guided munitions necessary to exploit its technical edge and minimize US and allied losses.

In short, US expeditionary capabilities for a single contingency depend heavily on strategic warning as well as prepositioning and support from US regional allies. Moreover, the constraints on US forces and readiness are changing the ability to fight more than one contingency at a time. At the time of the Bottom Up Review, US planners defined "near simultaneous" to mean a period of 45 to 60 days after the beginning of the first contingency. This definition focused on a relatively short time window in which the US would have deployed its forces for a first major regional contingency, and lift would be free to move forces for a second first major regional contingency before that lift was needed to move supplies and follow-on forces. It also assumed a very high degree of strategic warning and preparation, that the US would funded high readiness levels, and that the US would have almost all of the force improvements called for in the Bottom Up Review in place.

These assumptions always made the a strategy of fighting two "near simultaneous" major regional contingencies more of an exercise in political symbolism than serious war planning. The cuts in spending, modernization, forces, and readiness since the Bottom Up Review now mean, however, that "near simultaneous" is slowly slipping from a real-world gap of about six months between US ability to win in one contingency and fully deploy to another contingency, to a gap of roughly nine to 15 months depending on the seriousness of each contingency.

This growing inability to implement a strategy of being able to fight "two near simultaneous regional contingencies" scarcely means US military power is crippled, but it does mean that any analysis of the evolving US contingency capabilities in the Gulf must increasingly take into account the global limits on US military power, and the risk that US forces needed in the Gulf may be engaged in other contingencies.

Many US planners, including senior planners in the Joint Staff and the military staffs of the US services, believe that these cuts have effectively reduced the US to a one MRC strategy. They feel that the US is already in the process of adopting a single MRC, or "win-hold-win" strategy, in which the US would only be able to fight one major contingency at a time, and could do little more than conduct air and missile attacks in second— although the US has improved its ability to use air and missile power to strike at any aggressor during the "hold" phase of a second contingency. They feel that the only reason the US has not announced this change in strategy is the concern the Clinton Administration has that such an announcement would affect the 1996 election.

"Win-Hold-Win" and Strategic Warning

The fact that the US has almost certainly already been forced into a "win-hold-win" or "single MRC" strategy must also be kept in careful perspective. It can be argued that sizing US forces for two near simultaneous major regional contingencies is planning for a worst-case scenario, and that there is little probability that the US will have to fight major conflict in the Gulf and Korea at the same time.

It can also be argued that even if two crises do occur at the same time, the US could focus on the more serious threat and adopt an aggressive variant of a "win-hold-win" strategy in dealing with the less serious case. Even under worst-case conditions, the US should be able to bring powerful air and missile assets to bear in a Gulf contingency and to begin offensive attacks on enemy strategic and tactical targets during the "hold" phase of such a conflict.

The US may not always be able to "hold" in a worst-case contingency like an all-out Iraqi attack on northern Kuwait, or an Iranian grab of some strategic island or location in the Gulf. However, Iran and Iraq have no prospect of being able to attack with impunity or to see the US paralyzed or forced into a purely defensive role because of an involvement in a contingency or contingencies outside the Gulf region.

Modifying the Phases of Conflict

There also have been changes in US strategy and US forces which improve US war fighting capabilities in Southwest Asia. One of the most important changes US planners have made since the Bottom Up Review is to modify the objectives assigned to each phase of a war in the Gulf. They realize that future aggressors may not repeat Iraq's decision to stop at a given border and may advance much more quickly in an effort to create decisive "facts on the ground" before the US can react. As a result, the US is placing far more emphasis on decisive action during the "halt phase."

Rather than simply trying to check the enemy's advance during the "halt phase," US planners now envisage a campaign of aggressive engagement aimed at seriously degrading enemy military capabilities at the start of any enemy attack, and reducing the requirement for US forces during the build-up phase. This emphasis on decisive engagement has increased the US emphasis on early offensive air and missile strikes, including both strategic and tactical attacks on a potential enemy, on forward presence, and on rapidly deployable offensive strike forces.

This change in strategy and in the planned phases of US military action in a Gulf War allows the US to exploit one of the key lessons of the Gulf War: a strategic and tactical air and missile offensive could begin immediately, without waiting to win air superiority or to deploy the land forces necessary to commence an offensive AirLand battle. This change allows the US to exploit its steadily improving air and missile technology, and advantages like "stealth," "24 hour" air operations, greatly improved near real-time targeting, precision stand-off attack capability, and greatly improved anti-armor and hard-point attack capabilities. It reduces the risk of having to deal with fait accomplis and having to liberate friendly territory, and ensures that an aggressor will come under immediate strategic pressure in the form of attacks on homeland targets of critical value to an attacking nation's leadership. This exploitation of air and missile power is an essential complement and preface to the improvements that the US is making in its capabilities for the AirLand battle.

Force Improvements Since the Gulf War

There also have been important improvements in the capabilities of the forces the US can deploy forward to the Gulf and Southwest Asia. In spite of the cuts in the total size of US forces, the US has been able to react to many of the detailed lessons of the Gulf War, to make significant improvements in organization and training, and to improve "jointness" and its capability to conduct highly sophisticated combined operations.

The US has established a strong forward presence in the Gulf. In early 1996, the US had about 9,000 troops stationed on land, and another 15,000 sailors and marines deployed on 15–20 warships in or near the Gulf. These ships had up to 100 aircraft, and about 170 additional USAF aircraft were deployed in the region—including fighters, strike aircraft, tank killers, intelligence and electronic warfare aircraft. About 5,000 US government and contractor personnel were also in the region, supporting US arms sales and advisory missions to friendly Southern Gulf states.[53] These forces were supported by the US power projection capabilities discussed earlier.

Further, the US has made detailed force improvements in US equipment, support systems, tactics and training, and C⁴I systems which significantly improve its capability to fight in the Middle East and Southwest Asia. This progress is summarized in Table Seven. It is clear that

TABLE SEVEN   Force Improvements in US Capabilities Since Desert Storm

Increased Land Warfighting Capability

- Increased night warfighting capability with fielding of significant upgrades in numbers and types of night-vision devices for ground units.
- Increased survivability for M-1/M-1A1/M-1A2 tanks with improvements to anti-armor, and development of an M-1A2 upgrade program to provide improved sensor and C4I/BM capabilities.
- Fitting the Bradley with 108 explosive reactive armor tiles to reduce its vulnerability.
- Providing the AH-64 with the Longbow up-grade, a day-night and relatively long-range surveillance/targeting system, and "fire and forget" anti-tank missile capability against tanks and armor.
- Planned conversion of 180–380 Bradley M-2A2s into a new Fire Support Team (FIST) variant with an AN/TVQ-2 ground vehicle laser designator, an AN/TAS-4B TOW night sight, the Advanced Field Artillery Data System, and an inertial navigation and ring laser gyro system with a 80 meter CEP at a range of 10 kilometers. The FIST will replace the M-981 (M-113 based) fire support team vehicle with a much more capable weapons system.
- Improved precision navigation capability for Special Operations Force (SOF) helicopters (MH-60/MH-47) at extended ranges and for low-level flight in adverse weather.
- Improvements to lethality of Tube-launched Optically-tracked Wire-guided (TOW) and Hellfire missiles.
- Procurement of the V-22 to improve Marine Corps tactical mobility and assault capability, and of additional Blackhawks to improve US Army tactical mobility.
- Development of new "digital battlefield" concepts for deployment in the early 2000s to integrate US Army combined arms operations and provide near real-time situational awareness. US Army plans to spend $1.7 on battlefield digitization during FY1997–FY2002.
- Development of a new five year US Marine Corps program for Advanced Combat and Technology Demonstrations to improve force structures and weapons mixes for dispersed area combat, longer range engagements, urban warfare, and joint Navy-Marine Corps conduct of amphibious and land combat operations.[54]
- Procurement of a new family of medium tactical vehicles.

Increased Maritime Warfighting Capability

- Activation of the US Fifth Fleet on July 1, 1995, under the command of Vice Admiral Scott Redd. The Fifth Fleet is formally based at the port of Mina Sulman in Bahrain, and has a headquarters facility there. It is an operational command reporting to US Central Command (CENTCOM), with responsibility for an area of 10.5 million square miles, including the Red Sea, Arabian Sea, Gulf and Indian Ocean, The Fifth Fleet will include two nuclear power submarines, an

(*continues*)

TABLE SEVEN   (*continued*)

---

aircraft carrier battle group, and various support ships on a rotational basis. It has recently averaged a strength of about 15 ships.[55]

- Improved anti-air warfare capability with procurement of new AEGIS-equipped guided missile destroyers.
- Extended coastal patrol and interdiction operations by SOF forces with fielding of new Patrol Coastal ships.
- Significantly improved propulsion system of ships with conversion to gas turbine systems over conventional steam driven surface combatants.
- Increased Tomahawk lethality with upgrades to the missile range, launchers, and navigation systems. A total of $25 million is provided in FY1996 to accelerated Block IV upgrades to the Tomahawk missile which are designed to improve accuracy and allow for secondary target acquisition. An average of five DDG-51s equipped with the 90 cell vertical launch system (VLS) have entered the US fleet every year since 1994, and all deployed US submarines are to be equipped with cruise missiles.[56]
- Increased mine countermeasures capabilities with delivery of last Avenger-class minesweeper in 1994. US mine forces are converting from 19 poor quality Category B mobilization ships to 8 Category B mobilization ships and 15 active mine warfare ships.
- Merging of the Advanced Combat Direction System (ACDS) and Ship-Self Defense Capability/Quick Reaction Capability (SSDS/ORCC) into one integrated ship defense system to provide integrated detect-control-engage capabilities. The result will be a cooperative engagement capability (CEC) for all major US ship classes and E-2Cs to combine weapons and sensor control data in real time. Initial operating capability is expected in 1996–1997, with eventual deployment of over 183 systems.[57]
- Demonstrated capability to rapidly deploy 12 prepositioning ships in the Gulf as of September 1995.[58]
- Deployment of two modern mine countermeasure vessels, the USS Ardent and USS Dextrous, to the Fifth Fleet in the Gulf in March 1996.[59]
- Development of new carrier support procedures to increase carrier aircraft sortie rate and sortie sustainment capabilities.[60]

Increased Air Warfighting Capacity

- Revision of air warfare doctrine to stress the immediate use of strategic and tactical strikes to halt the enemy advance and attack key strategic and tactical targets in enemy territory using advanced strike aircraft and cruise missiles. This means planning for air-missile campaigns that may precede the AirLand battle and shifting to the offensive even during the "halt phase" of a conflict.
- Spending $800 million to upgrade Airborne Warning and Air Control Systems during FY1997–FY1998.
- Development and operational testing of the US Navy Cooperative Engagement Capability (CEC) to coordinate target data for US Navy, Army, Marine Corps,

---

(*continues*)

TABLE SEVEN   *(continued)*

and Air Force joint air defense command and control, to allow each ship in a disperse battle group to simultaneously track and target enemy missiles, and to coordinate sea and land-based anti-air missiles. The first installation in a carrier battle group will occur in the fall of 1997. Some $300 million is requested for procurement of the system in FY1997. The CEC may be integrated into the AWACS during 1998–2001.[61]

- Improved precision strike capability with increased number of F-15E/Block 40 F-16s equipped with Low Altitude Navigation Targeting Infrared for Night (LANTIRN) upgrade completed in 1994. These platforms, combined with F-117s, provide nearly 400 precision laser-guided munition airframes and have significantly increased our night fighting capability.
- The Advanced Medium Range Air-to-Air Missile (AMRAAM) has been fielded. It provides F-15s, F-16s, and F-18s radar missiles with longer range over the AIM-7, and its launch and leave capability enhances survival on the battlefield. The AMRAAM gives the F-16Cs their first radar missile capability—vastly increasing their lethality and survivability.
- Improved anti-armor cluster munition capability with initial deliveries of the Sensor Fused Weapon (SFW). Each bomblet has an infrared sensor to detect tank engines and an accurate penetrating warhead. This weapon will give all USAF fighters and bombers a precision capability to kill moving or static armor formations. US studies have indicated that the Sensor Fused Weapon will allow air forces to make a major improvement in their ability to halt an armored attack in the Gulf region, and to halt enemy armored advances even when there is too little warning to deploy prepositioned land forces. A total of 400 Sensor Fused Weapons will be procured in FY1997.
- Air Force is procuring the first 1,085 Joint Direct Attack Munitions (JDAM, out of a planned buy of 74,000, in FY1997. These weapons will improve precision stand-off strike capability for the F-15E, F-16, F-22, B-52, B-1B, and B-2.
- Block 50 F-16s have been modified to employ High Speed Anti-Radiation Missiles (HARM) to improve their capability to perform the suppression of enemy air defense mission and fill the gap created by retirement of F-4Gs.
- Award of the Joint Air Strike Tactical (JAST) fighter development contract in January 1996 for delivery in the post-2010 time-frame.

Increased Mobility and Prepositioning

- The US Maritime Prepositioning Force now consists of three Maritime Prepositioning Squadrons (MPS), each of which is able to support a Marine Expeditionary Force (MEF) of approximately 15,000 personnel for 30 days. There are three prepositioning ships with Air Force stocks (largely ammunition) and five Army prepositioning ships with port-opening equipment, ammunition, rations, and other sustainment stocks. The Army will have one brigade afloat set at sea on Ready Reserve Fleet (RRF) ships by the end of FY1997. The Army

(continues)

TABLE SEVEN   *(continued)*

demonstrated the effectiveness of this maritime prepositioning system in October 1994.

- New prepositioned (prepo) stocks significantly reduced closure time and space requirements for lift to theater, providing increased firepower to the CINC sooner. A heavy brigade prepo set in Kuwait (AWR-5) is nearly complete. The Army heavy brigade set afloat prepo (AWR-3) has been fielded and met all performance criteria set forth in the Defense Planning Guidance. Plans are in-place for positioning a brigade set in Qatar, but funding is an issue.
- The C-17 is being fielded, providing direct delivery of outsize cargo (C-5 loads to C-139 airfields) and will augment the aging C-141/C-5 fleet. The Department of Defense decided to procure a total of 120 planes in November, 1995.
- Ready Reserve Force sealift improvements include addition of 12 additional roll-on/roll-off vessels to augment the strategic sealift resources.
- USCENTCOM has a developed a Total Asset Visibility (TAV) system to track theater assets of equipment and logistics throughout the theater in near real time. Deployment of this system should correct major problems in locating in-theater and reinforcing stocks and equipment experienced during the Gulf War, and allow more efficient use of assets.

Command, Control, Communication, Computers, and Intelligence

- Fielding MILSTAR satellites to provide secure, survivable communications to both strategic and tactical warfighting forces during all levels of conflict. MILSTAR follow-on program in development.
- Procurement of 10 Joint Surveillance Target Attack Reconnaissance Systems aircraft, beginning with two aircraft in FY1997, to track and target the movement of vehicles and other platforms on the battlefield.
- Improvement of the permanently installed Southwest Asia Defense Information Infrastructure (SWADII) and development of the rapidly deployable Tactical Contingency Communications Equipment-Central Area (TCCE-CA) to provide C4I/BM capabilities for joint operations in the Gulf area. These improvements are reinforced by other improvements to the Defense Satellite Communications System (DSCS), UHF follow-on satellite program, and MILSTAR. In addition, the US has developed the Joint Deployable Intelligence Support System (JDISS) and improved the theater capabilities of the Joint Worldwide Intelligence Communications System (JWICS).
- Improved systems for planning and executing joint air operations with fielding of the Contingency Theater Automated Planning System (CTAPS). Improves centralized control over fixed-wing assets for maximum effectiveness and standardizes the format for disseminating the Air Tasking Order.
- A National Imagery and Mapping Agency (NIMA) is to begin operations in October 1996. The NIMA is intended to provide much more rapid exploitation and dissemination of imagery and to provide improved near real-time targeting capability. It will include the Defense Mapping Agency (DMA), Central Im-

(continues)

TABLE SEVEN (*continued*)

agery Office (CIO), and National Photographic Interpretation Center (NPIC), and dissemination and interpretation assets from the Defense Airborne Reconnaissance Program and National Reconnaissance Program.

- The Joint Deployable Intelligence System (JDISS) is installed at all major sites in Riyadh and Bahrain, allowing for secure transmission of data to coordinate the CINC's war plans. Combined with fielding of the Joint Worldwide Intelligence Communication System (JWICS), USCINCCENT could tie together national, theater, and tactical intelligence systems. The result is a robust, seamless intelligence flow using compatible systems down to the component commander and his forces.
- Battle Damage Assessment (BDA) doctrine which standardizes terminology, procedures, and training have been developed to improve the operational ability to collect and exploit timely imagery and other intelligence information regarding the target, and developing an effective, common methodology for assessing damage. DIA and the Joint Staff have developed a concept for providing timely BDA during military operations. A BDA cell has been established in the National Military Joint Intelligence Center in the Pentagon to provide a single, fused, all-source, national-level assessment to the supported command. Regular exercises test these procedures.
- USCINCCENT development and coordination of new BDA procedures throughout the intelligence community. The development of deployable airborne collection platforms with enhanced capabilities and the doctrine to better integrate them into the BDA system has increased effectiveness. Building on joint intelligence doctrine, USCENTCOM has refined its theater intelligence architecture and developed its own CENTCOM tactics, techniques, and procedures to document joint approaches to command the component intelligence activities and relationships.
- The interoperability and efficiency of the C4I systems has been increased with the fielding of the Global Command and Control System (GCCS), which provides the commanders from all components a common picture of the battlefield.
- The Defense Satellite Communications System (DSCS) has been upgraded to allow larger bandwidth connections to the theater.
- Procuring new space-based infra-red system program to track missiles from space.
- While no telephone switch infrastructure existed prior to Desert Storm, over 250 Defense Switch Networks have now come into the theater from CONUS, Japan, and Germany.
- Procurement of large numbers of Single Channel Ground and Airborne Radio systems (SINCGARS) for improved tactical communications.

Organizational Changes Have Placed
Greater Emphasis on Regional Commands and Joint Training

- Activation of the USACOM in October 1993. Facilitates the identification, structuring, joint training, and joint preparation of CONUS-based forces.

(*continues*)

TABLE SEVEN   *(continued)*

- Activation of the Joint Warfighting Center in July 1993. Assists joint force commanders in training their forces and for development of joint doctrine.
- Joint doctrine has been developed and documented for close air support, fire support, command and control, joint air operations, and many other mission areas. This doctrine has been integrated into joint training and exercises.
- CINC-sponsored exercises have transitioned from global to regional scenarios. These exercises have increased in number and frequency, but decreased in size and scope.
- Exercise trends include increased use of modeling and simulation, enhancing military relations and interoperability with allies/coalition, containerization of ammunition and unit equipment, exercising prepositioned equipment, and special forces participation.
- The IMET program is being steadily strengthened to train officers from the Southern Gulf states in joint operations and the US now deploys more than 800 military personnel in Security Assistance Organizations (SAOs), Technical Assistance Field Teams (TAFTs), and Mobile Training Teams (MTTs) in the US-CENTCOM area. This is steadily improving Southern Gulf capability for joint and coalition warfare. These efforts are reinforced by the expansion of SOC-CENT joint special operations forces which also work with Southern Gulf forces.

Source: Adapted from material provided by the Office of the Chairman of the Joint Chiefs of Staff, Department of Defense, and USCENTCOM.

each military service has reacted to its experience during Desert Shield and Desert Storm, and the lessons of the Gulf War.

The US has already demonstrated some of the benefits of these force improvements in Bosnia. While the US did continue to experience serious problems in the coordination of National Technical Means within its intelligence community, it achieved a substantially higher level of accuracy in precision air strikes. Its performance reflected training by simulating missions before their execution, better air defense weapons suppression planning and strikes, better resources in terms of laser illuminators and advanced attack avionics, more effective use of daytime strikes, better reconnaissance and targeting and the use of advanced UAVs, substantial improvements in the C^4I systems and organization used to task strikes, use of improved Tomahawk missiles and some types of precision ordnance, and improved battle damage assessment.[62]

The US also is scarcely the only power which has encountered resource and modernization problems. Iran and Iraq currently have much smaller total forces than the US used in sizing the nominal threat for a major regional contingency in the Bottom Up Review, and it seems likely that the US will retain the ability to intervene decisively in the Gulf against any current conventional threat posed by Iran or Iraq.

Iran has faced a continuing economic crisis during most of the 1990s, and its military spending levels have been much lower than the US anticipated at the time of the BUR. As a result, Iran's conventional modernization has been limited—although Iran has been able to improve important aspects of its air and armored forces, and its threat to maritime traffic in the Gulf. Iraq has been cut off from military imports ever since August 1990, and has had virtually no oil exports. In spite of efforts to reorganize its forces and expand its military industries, Iraq's overall capabilities have declined steadily since its initial period of recovery following the Gulf War.

Uncertainties in Future
US Power Projection Capabilities

These contradictory trends make it extremely difficult to draw a balance between the impact of the cuts in the total size of US forces and long-term readiness and the improvements the US has made in the ability of its remaining forces to fight in the Gulf area. It is clear, however, that US capabilities in the Gulf will be shaped largely by how the US deals with the key military uncertainties that affect the size, readiness, and modernization of the forces it relies on in deploying to Southwest Asia. These uncertainties are listed in Table Eight.

There is another set of uncertainties that is inherent in the very nature of the US search for force improvement to execute a "revolution in military affairs." Each improvement in US capabilities creates the paradox that the US is potentially increasing the tactical, technical, training, and sustainability problems it faces in coalition warfare at a time when it has a growing need for such support from its allies.

The US has already bought a much more sophisticated mix of long-range conventional strike assets, air superiority assets, "smart" munitions, and C⁴I/BM assets than it possessed during the Gulf War. All of these assets contribute to high technology methods of combat and to an intensity of operations that either requires allied forces to have similar capabilities or to be "compartmented" in ways which ensure that they do not interfere with US operations or present problems in terms of friendly fire.

The Coalition-oriented rhetoric of the Gulf War has disguised the fact that many allied contributions had little war fighting value, while others presented almost as many complications as they were worth. The Saudi Air Force, for example, was the only Coalition air force with the technical sophistication to carry out forward air defense operations in combined warfare with the USAF—in fact, the USN F-14s lacked the proper C⁴I assets to be integrated into the air defense operations over the Kuwaiti Theater of Operations.

TABLE EIGHT   Major Uncertainties in US Power Projection Capabilities in the
Gulf

- *US Army force strength:* Current US Army force plans call for an end-strength of 495,000 men and women in FY1997. The Army faces such serious funding constraints, however, that it may actually have to cut its personnel to levels below 475,000 to generate funds for modernization. This would force it to hollow out some aspects of its planned 10 division force structure, with an inevitable impact on readiness and power projection capabilities. Further, the Army could be forced into further cuts in future years.
- *US Army readiness for power projection:* The US Army now plans its power projection capabilities around its Contingency Corps (XVIII Airborne Corps) which consists primarily of three light divisions (the 82nd Airborne Division, 101st Air Assault Division, and 10th Mountain Division) and one heavy division (the 24 Mechanized Infantry Division). The US Army has a goal of being able to deploy the entire four division corps to the Gulf in 75 days by 1998, and one light and two heavy divisions in 30 days.[63] The Army also has a Reinforcing Corps (III Corps), which consists of five divisions. Three of these divisions, however, are active divisions that require Army Reserve and National Guard Round outs, and two are reserve component divisions. The Army also has some separate brigades and additional ranger and special forces units.

  The US Army Contingency Corps consists primarily of light forces, is a relatively limited land component to fight a high-intensity armored battle in a major regional conflict, and the capability of the Reinforcing Corps to fight such an armored conflict without more than three to five months of prior preparation and deployment is uncertain. The Army also faces problems in supporting these forces. It is modernizing much of its equipment, but at a far slower rate than was planned in 1990, and many important programs have been slipped or canceled—including the armored gun system. The US Army has also had to cut back on stock levels and munitions modernization plans. These cuts mean a significant cut in the technical superiority or "edge" the US Army can deploy in future regional contingencies and they have been accompanied by significant cuts in the longer term aspects of readiness. At the same time, it is unclear that the US Army is fully funded to modernize and improve its ability to rapidly deploy units from casernes to sea and air ports, or to conduct the kind of advanced large-scale air-missile and AirLand training needed to be fully ready for a contingency in the Gulf.[64]

  In the near-term, the Army's logistic preparation capability for two MRCs appears questionable. The Army has only 700 of the 1,945 rail cars it needs to move Force Package 1—the first US heavy division—to a port. It also lacks the container handling equipment needed to load and unload rail cars, and the $13.5 million earmarked to support US sealift capability with the floating cranes, tugs, and causeway systems needed to facilitate the loading an unloading of equipment on to and off of large roll-on/roll-off ships has been cut from

(continues)

TABLE EIGHT   *(continued)*

the Army's five year plan. Only some of these shortfalls are addressed in the present FY1996–2001 force plan.[65]

Equally important, the Army has been forced to rely on National Guard and Army Reserve combat support and service support units for deployment of its contingency forces although these can present serious political problems in calling up the necessary reserves, and many proved to have C-4 or C-5 readiness during Desert Shield.

- *US Marine Corps capabilities for mid to high-intensity conflict:* The Marine Corps found during the Gulf War that it lacked the heavy armor for high-intensity regional conflicts, lacked sufficient artillery firepower and mobility, needed improved air support capability, needed improved tactical airlift, and needed at least one additional prepositioning ship per MEB. The Marine Corps has obtained some additional M-1A1 tanks from the Army and has upgraded the avionics and precision strike capabilities of its AV-8Bs and F/A-18s. It has not, however, acquired the number of tanks it originally sought, may see plans to modernize its AAVs slip by half a decade or more, and must rely on towed 155 mm artillery that must be supplemented by the deployment of supporting US Army units in mid to high-intensity combat. It continues to experience major delays in modernizing its tactical lift and will not acquire an added prepositioning ship for each MEB. Equally important, the Gulf War demonstrated that the USMC lacked the sustainment capability for intensive land warfare. At present, the Marine Corps can only sustain about 1.5 to 2 of its three MEFs in intense combat for more than 30–45 days.

- *US Carrier strength:* US commitments in other areas and declines in readiness and carrier strength have made it progressively hard to deploy a carrier in the Gulf, and two carriers in the Gulf and Mediterranean/Red Sea areas. The US Navy has increasing been forced to leave gaps in carrier coverage, although the US has compensated in part by deploying USAF fighters to Bahrain and Jordan.[66]

- *US sealift:* US sealift plays a critical role in deployment to the Gulf, although sheer distance inevitably limits the speed of reaction. It is 8,600 sea miles and 20+ days sailing time from the US east coast to the Gulf through the Suez Canal and 11,400 sea miles and 26+ days sailing time around Africa.

There are major ongoing improvements in US sealift. The US Military Sealift Command now has a total of 224 ships, including 12 in the special mission support force, 170 in the strategic sealift force, and 42 in the naval auxiliary force. The core of this capability is the rapid deployment force, which includes 33 afloat prepositioning ship (12 Army, 4 USN, 13 USMC, and 4 USAF). The US also has a surge capability of eight fast sealift ship (FSS) and 22 roll on/roll off (RO-RO) ships in the Ready Reserve Force (RRF).[67]

The most rapidly deployable elements of US sealift include the Army prepositioning ships (AR-3), which include seven RO-ROs from the RRF, one auxiliary crane ship, three barge carriers (LASH), and one heavy preposition-

(continues)

ing ship (HLPS). This force can carry about 40% of the equipment needed to deploy and sustain one brigade, and each RO-RO ship can either carry the equipment for an armored battalion (51 M-1A1 tanks) or the equipment for a mechanized battalion (72 M-2 Bradleys.) The total force can carry about 40% of the total equipment load for two armored battalions, two mechanized battalions, and the required transportation, engineer, supply, medical, and maintenance units. At present, 4 RO-ROs, 3 LASH, and 1 HLPS out of this total are deployed in the Indian Ocean and homeported in Diego Garcia, and the US is seeking to homeport the rest in Thailand.[68]

The four Navy ships include three tankers and one 500 bed hospital. The 13 USMC ships include three squadrons, each of which support one Marine Expeditionary Force of about 16,000 men. They each hold about 30 M-1A1 tanks (being increased to 58), 109 AAVs, 30 M-198 howitzers, 289 5 ton trucks, 530 HUMMWVs, 10 LCM-8s, and 35 causeway sections. The four USAF ships provide sustainment and ammunition.[69]

These capabilities meet many important requirements, but even the rapidly deployable elements are still underfunded. The US Army currently can only preposition about 40% of a full 2X2 combat brigade and combat support/combat service support slice. It does not have the ability to provide 30 days of sealift for sustainment of its 4 division contingency force. This will require funding of eight LMSRs to replace the present RO-ROs, two container ships, and an additional HLPS. The total present surge capability of the MSC is also only about 45% of the total requirement called for in US mobility requirements. To meet its requirements, the US must acquire 19 large medium-speed roll on/roll off (LMSR) ships during FY1995–FY2001 and two more container ships. The total requirement for the RRF is 36 RO-RO ships. The US had 17 before Desert Shield, is acquiring 12, and needs 7 more. The US is also badly underfunding the readiness of its RRF ships, and 45 ships were without maintenance funds in FY1995.

- *US airlift:* The Gulf is 7,000 air miles and 24 hours flight time from the US. However, the US cut its total requirement for strategic airlift from 57 MTM/D to 52 MTM/D during the Bottom Up Review. Even so, there is little probability that it will meet its goals. The USAF's Mobility Command has indicated that even with the full mobilization of the Air Reserve Command and the Civil Reserve Air Fleet (CRAF), it can move only 48.8 MTM/D.[70] The current US fleet consists of 104 C-5s, 199 C-141s, 12 C-17s, and 415 C-130s. The US also has an aerial refueling fleet of 478 KC-135s and 54 KC-10s.[71] The C-141 has only about eight more years of useful life and the USAF must deal with the near-term implications of a combination of the aging of the C-141, delays in the C-17, and cost problems in procuring the C-17 and other lift aircraft.

    USAF plans call for procurement of 120 C-17s, but still indicate that US strategic and tactical airlift will be limited to less than 90% of the current requirement until the end of the present planning period (2020), even if the C-17

(*continues*)

TABLE EIGHT   *(continued)*

is fully funded and a new aircraft type is purchased to supplement the C-17. The US also has no attrition reserve of lift aircraft, and its current plans make no allowance for any peacetime or wartime attrition of USAF lift aircraft for nearly the next quarter century. Current plans also conceal the fact that the USAF only has enough major long lead spare for its strategic lift aircraft for about 45 days of high-intensity wartime operations. It seems likely that the US will face major lift capacity problems by the end of the 1990s, and may be reduced to about 80% of its present requirement.[72]

- *Firepower for light divisions:* These developments are occurring at a time when the US Army is becoming steadily more dependent on airlift to rapidly move firepower. The cancellation of the US Army Armored Gun System (AGS)—which was to replace the obsolete M-551 Sheridan in the 82nd Airborne Division—has forced the Army to consider rapid air deployment of the Bradley as a substitute. While the C-17 can carry one M-1A2 Abrams, it requires at least a 2,800 foot hard runway to do so and runway length increases with temperature and altitude. The Bradley weights less than half the weight of the M-1A2, and a C-17 can carry up to three Bradleys if equipment is taken off them to reduce their weight. The question is whether the TOW missiles and 25 mm chain gun on the Bradley can substitute for the 105 mm gun on the AGS. US light divisions may lack the tank-killing power and mobility they need.[73]

- *US bomber forces:* Congressional efforts to procure more B-2s have delayed the upgrading of the US bomber force and have left questions about the ability of the B-2 and B-1B to meet their goals for delivery of smart weapons like the Sensor Fused Weapon with the lethality projected in US plans. The B-1 is now limited to delivery of a maximum of 84 500-pound dumb bombs. It will acquire the technical capability to drop Sensor Fused Weapons at the end of 1996, as well as combined effects munitions and mines. However, the supporting precision strike systems will not be deployed before 2000 at the earliest, and plans to upgrade the inadequate ALQ-161 electronic warfare suite on the B-1B remain uncertain.[74] The precision conventional strike capabilities of the B-2, and operational validation of the very high lethality rates projected for B-2 strikes, remains theoretical and is not yet supported by the sophisticated targeting and C^4I/BM systems necessary to achieve such lethality.[75]

- *US air and missile strike capabilities:* Two major issues are unresolved in current US force plans which will have a major impact on US capabilities to conduct long-range air strikes. The US does not have a stable or credible plan for bomber modernization, and for providing the advanced munitions, targeting, and C^4I/BM capabilities needed to operate any given mix of the B-52/B-1, and B-2 in combat. At the same time, the US Air Force and US Navy have canceled the A-12 and A-X, the USN is withdrawing the A-6 from service in 1997, and the USAF is debating withdrawing the F-111. Even if the Joint Advanced Strike Aircraft (JAST) program should be funded, the US will have no plans to deliver

(continues)

a new long-range strike-attack aircraft that can be used by carrier aviation, the Marine Corps, and the USAF until well after the year 2010.[76]

The US is upgrading its cruise missile and stand-off strike missiles. Key new systems like the JSOW and SLAM-ER are on schedule, and the TLAM is being upgraded. The TSSAM cruise missile program has been canceled, however, and funds seem likely to be lacking for adequate procurement of the JSOW, SLAM-ER, and TLAM.

The US has partially compensated for these problems (a) by improving the strike/attack capabilities of existing aircraft like the AV-8B, F-15E, F-16, and F/A-18C/D, (b) by procuring the F/A-18E/F for US carrier forces, and (c) by providing a stealth strike capability for the F-22 air superiority fighter. The fact remains, however, that there is no coherence or stability to US plans to improve long-range strike capabilities, and these capabilities will improve at only a fraction of the rate planned in 1990. The current US force plan conceals role and mission debates, inter-service debates, and program uncertainties that badly need to be resolved.

- *US Navy and amphibious lift capabilities:* The downsizing of the US Navy and the potential block obsolescence of some aspects of US amphibious lift create significant potential problems in terms of maintaining forward deployed carrier task forces and adequate amphibious assault capabilities. These problems have been increased by the long delay in modernizing Marine Corps tactical airlift, and the need for improved vertical lift capability to counter the improved mine warfare capabilities in areas like the Gulf. These problems could significantly affect US capabilities in a high-intensity regional conflict in the Gulf, and USN studies project a potential problem in amphibious lift retirements and modernization after 2005, although current procurement plans for the LPD-17 class ships would provide a full capability to lift the assault echelons of 2.5 MEBs when these ships are fully delivered, and the USN adopted an Amphibious Enhancement Plan in August, 1994 that calls for interim measures to avoid a gap while the LPD-17 class is being procured. This plan would retain LSTs and LKAs in the Naval and Military Sealift Command Reserve Force previously scheduled to be decommissioned or sold.

- *US mine warfare capabilities:* The funding of US mine warfare capabilities remains uncertain, although total US Navy future year defense plan funding of mine warfare programs now totals approximately $4 billion, and $104 million more was added in FY1996. The US Navy is currently focusing on shallow water assault breaching, distributed explosive technology, and remote mine-hunting systems, and has accelerated the airborne mine neutralization system. It is continuing to fund upgrades to mechanical sweep systems, unmanned underwater vehicles, remote mine hunting systems and the Quickstrike mine.[77] The Navy, however, has sought at least $40 million more per year for mine warfare in FY1997 and FY1997 to speed up the deployment of mine countermeasure capabilities. It is seeking more funds for mine coun-

(*continues*)

TABLE EIGHT   (*continued*)

termeasure ships, airborne mine hunting helicopters, divers for mine clearing, route surveys of ocean lanes and a mine warfare data base on underwater obstacles, new C^4I/BM systems for mine warfare, mine tracking systems, and deployment of the Remote Minehunting System and Magic Lantern laser mine detection system.[78]

- *Friendly fire capabilities:* The US is only making limited progress in solving its identification of friend or foe (IFF) or "friendly fire" problems. While a number of interesting technical options exist, the Pentagon's Joint Combat Identification Office (JCIDO) is just beginning to bring these to the demonstration phase, and equip aircraft like the A-10 and F-16 with real time data links to US and friendly ground troops.

- *Target acquisition and analysis/battle damage assessment capability (BDA):* In spite of USCENTCOM and other US efforts to improve target acquisition and BDA capability, US intelligence officers and some air war planners feel that the Department of Defense has failed to react adequately to the lessons of the Gulf War in developing improved regional capabilities for targeting and battle damage assessment capability to support US C^4I/BM capabilities and improved precision strike capabilities. They feel the US has failed to develop adequate regional strike plans against Iran and Iraq, that many target acquisition systems lag far beyond schedule, and that the improvements made in BDA that have been made so far are more bureaucratic cosmetics than real improvements.

- *Readiness and sustainment:* In spite of Department of Defense claims that readiness is not declining, each of the services privately state that current funds are not adequate and that the cost of peacekeeping and other partially funded unprogrammed operations continues to force declines in training, combat and support unit readiness, stock levels, depot and major maintenance, and refits. Many air, naval, and Marine Corps units are forced to deploy much longer than is desirable, and this is stressing manpower as well as equipment.

- *Theater missile defense systems:* The US has invested heavily in the development of theater missile defense systems like the Patriot Advanced Capability 3, the Theater High Altitude Area Defense (THAAD), and Navy lower tier program. It has not, however, been able to create a stable deployment program. The wide area capabilities of its systems are now limited by US mishandling of negotiations with Russia over the ABM treaty, and initiatives to create a "net" of land-based surface-to-air missile in the Southern Gulf countries have made only limited progress. This means that US deployment of effective ATBM capabilities may lag behind Iranian missile deployments, and that progress in creating an effective joint US-Southern Gulf surface-to-air missiles/ATBM capability may be limited or inadequate.[79]

- *Chemical and Biological Warfare Capabilities:* Development and/or deployment of improved detection systems, protective gear and equipment, decontamination gear, and vaccines/medical systems lags badly behind the goals US forces set after the Gulf War.[80]

(*continues*)

TABLE EIGHT   (*continued*)

- *Procurement cut-backs and delays:* Secretary of Defense William Perry warned in January 1996, that the US could be forced into significant additional force cuts if Congress did not fund the $50–60 billion for weapons modernization called for the FY1997–FY2001 defense program. However, the defense procurement request for the FY1997 budget was only $39.9 billion out of the total budget request of $242.6 billion. This was the lowest procurement request in real dollars since 1990, and only 60% of the funding level at the height of the Cold War. It effectively deferred any effort to support the modernization of US forces until FY1998, and then created a FYDP which calls for real procurement spending to rise to $60.1 billion in FY2001, a rise of 40%. This kind of annual budgetary delay in badly needed modernization, and unrealistic rise in future spending, was called the "rolling get well" when US forces progressively deteriorated after Vietnam. Such budgeting raises severe doubts about the credibility of those modernization programs that are in the US FYDP, and makes a US two MRC strategy even less credible.[81]

US air units provided virtually all of the mass and decisive force that shaped the outcome of Desert Storm. If one counts only shooter and combat support sorties for fixed wing aircraft, the USAF flew 57% of the 92,517 sorties in Desert Storm. The US Navy flew 18.5%, and the USMC flew 10.8%, and all US forces flew a total of 86.3%. The RSAF flew 5.4%, the RAF flew 4.1%, the French Air Force flew 1.5%, the Canadian Air Force flew 1.0%, the Kuwaiti Air Force flew 0.8%, the Bahraini Air Force flew 0.3%, the Italian Air Force flew 0.2%, and Qatar and the UAE each flew less than 0.1%.[82]

US forces flew nearly 90% of all strike-attack sorties, and nearly 85% of all strike, attack, and air defense sorties. US air forces dominated every aspect of reconnaissance, electronic warfare, and command and control activity. They flew 90% of all reconnaissance missions, 96% of all command and control missions, and 97% of all electronic warfare missions. With the exception of the RAF, no allied air force made a significant contribution to the air offensive. Allied sorties were generally directed against low-priority static targets, and allied aircraft lacked the avionics and munitions required to achieve the proper lethality and survivability. Even the revised Tornado-Buccaneer force had significant C⁴I/BM integration problems in operating with US attack aircraft.

The US was forced to supply most of the theater-wide C⁴I/BM links for Coalition forces. The US Defense Satellite Communications System (DSCS) furnished about 75% of intra-theater connectivity during Desert Storm. The US provided virtually all satellite and advanced intelligence collection capability, and still experienced serious problems in the secure dissemination of such data to its own forces—much less its allies. Britain and Saudi Arabia were the only nations with full access to most threat data.

The US provided the bulk of the heavy armor and artillery committed to Desert Storm, and Britain proved to be the only European power able and willing to provide significant tank strength. The US also experienced serious problems in operating with Coalition land forces. The Egyptian forces faltered twice and played no significant role in the land battle. French forces reacted slowly and did not meet their objectives even with substantial US reinforcement and aid. US and British forces had significant C⁴I/BM integration problems, which only added to the confusion affecting the direction of the British advance once Britain had achieved its major mission of securing the flank of the US "left hook" and had crossed the gorge of Al Batin.

In spite of the much publicized deployment of naval contingents from the smaller NATO states and France, these forces contributed nothing to Desert Storm. Britain and the US provided all of the operational naval forces in the upper Gulf. In spite of the fact that several European powers sent mine clearing forces, only British mine forces led the way into combat. Every other Coalition naval contingent stayed safely out of harm's way.

In many cases, the US and/or Saudi Arabia were forced to provide much or most of the support required for smaller Gulf forces, and substantial intra-theater air or land lift. For example, Britain could provide commercial sea-lift, but not airlift. British forces had to make use of US C-5 transports, and British commercial cargo aircraft—including 38 Belfast sorties, 30 Tristar sorties, 23 Guppy sorties, three B-747 sorties, and 186 B-707 and DC-8 sorties from British owned aircraft. Britain also had to use C-130 flights flown by the Belgian, Portuguese, and Spanish Air Forces and chartered commercial aircraft. These commercial charters included one Aeroflot, AN-124 heavy lift aircraft sortie, 23 Sabena DC sorties, 28 US DC-8 sorties, 88 Romanian B-707 sorties, 30 Cathay Pacific B-747 sorties, 20 Evergreen Airways B-747 sorties, and 59 DC-8 and B-707 sorties by British owned, but foreign registered aircraft. Finally, Britain made use of two Kuwaiti C-130s, and all the Kuwaiti 747s that had escaped the Iraqi invasion.

These problems do not prevent allied European and Gulf forces from playing an important role in coalition missions that are relatively repetitive or static in nature, or which do not require the intensity of "24 hour" high-technology warfare. Bosnia has demonstrated that the changes to US forces scarcely preclude coalition operations. There are many contingencies which do not require the intensity of combat and integration of tactics, training, and technology the US is developing for mid and high-intensity conflict. Such contingencies include most peace-making, deterrent or demonstrative operations, and low-intensity combat operations.

At the same time, the US plans to make far more intense use of advanced C⁴I/BM than it did at the time of the Gulf War. It is emphasizing the near real-time fusion of all aspects of its C⁴I/BM systems in joint operations—virtually all of which require compatible technology, training, and tactics and which attempt to substitute force quality for force quantity. The US approach to war fighting is becoming more and more complex. Armies that do not adopt advanced digital battle management systems of the kind being developed by the US Army, and which do not have compatible sensors and mobility, will present more problems. Air forces that are not trained in AWACS/JSTARS/ABCCC operations will have less value. Joint forces that lack overall C⁴I/BM and joint training capabilities will present growing problems.

The US will have progressively fewer lift and sustainability resources to make up for the gaps in coalition force capabilities. It will progressively speed up the rate of offensive air operations in the early phase of battle against a major opponent. This means intensifying the sophistication of operations from the start of a conflict.

As a result, US forces are evolving in directions which may make it more and more difficult for moderate technology forces to act as a full partner in sophisticated main-battle operations, and which make it difficult for even advanced technology forces to act as a full partner unless they have fully compatible secure communications, data processing, C⁴I/BM systems, and training.

A great deal of NATO, Atlantic, GCC, and US rhetoric tends to "sloganize" war fighting capability and ignore the fact that most NATO European and Gulf combat units are moderate technology forces that are losing operational compatibility with the US. Further, it is becoming progressively harder to predict the real-world path that both US and allied forces will take as they react to the steady pressure to reduce defense expenditures. There is a serious risk that many of the technological "force multipliers" the US relies upon to try to compensate for force cuts, may turn into "force dividers" or "force limiters" in many forms of coalition warfare.

Uncertainties in Future US Contingency Capabilities

Finally, there are uncertainties that are contingency dependent. They are the inevitable result of the geography of the Gulf, and its dependence on the Southern Gulf states to participate in many aspects of their own defense. No US force posture can deal with every risk, and the overall strength of US forces relative to Iran and Iraq is not always the critical issue. There are several contingency capabilities where the US will continue to face problems, regardless of how it resolves the uncertainties in Table Eight:

- *A Sudden Iraqi Attack on Kuwait City:* Kuwait and Kuwait City remain vulnerable to a sudden Iraqi attack in which the Republican Guards and/or heavy regular Iraqi units invade Kuwait with only minimal preparation and warning. In spite of the improvements in US power projection capabilities, it is only about 80 to 120 kilometers from the Iraqi border to the edge of Al Jahrah and Kuwait City. Unless US prepositioned land forces and a significant number of Kuwaiti and other Arab land forces are positioned to screen the border and defend at the Mutlah pass north of Al Jahrah, it is unlikely that air power alone can halt a determined Iraqi force, particularly if that force uses some cover like an exercise to limit strategic warning. Once an Iraqi force penetrated into Kuwait City, it would be extremely difficult to dislodge—particularly if it held the Kuwaiti people hostage. The US would face severe limitations in using use air and artillery firepower.
- *An Iraqi Attack on Kuwait and Eastern Saudi Arabia:* There is little doubt that a combination of US, Kuwaiti, and Saudi forces could defeat any Iraqi invasion in the near to mid-term. There is also no question that the US could carry out devastating air and missile attacks on Iraq in reprisal for such an invasion within days after the Iraqi attack began. If Iraq was willing to take these risks, however, it could almost certainly occupy a substantial part of Kuwait and penetrate into Saudi Arabia before a combination of allied air and land power could halt an Iraqi invasion. Iraq might not only be able to take Al Jahrah and Kuwait City hostage, but also may be able to occupy Saudi cities and towns like Ar'ar, Rafha, and Khafji. Such a "hostage war" would involve massive risks for Iraq, and almost certain eventual defeat, but Iraq has made similar mistakes twice in the recent past. The US would need substantial support from Kuwaiti, Saudi, and other Gulf forces to minimize Iraqi success, and much would depend on both warning and immediate reaction to that warning.
- *Iranian pressure or attacks on Kuwait:* Iran demonstrated during the Iran-Iraq War that it could carry out terrorist attacks and assassination attempts in Kuwait using Iranian residents and/or Shi'ite Kuwaitis. It conducted threatening air movements and fired anti-ship missiles from the area around Nahr e-Qasr at naval targets near Kuwait's coast. These kinds of low-level attacks must be dealt with largely by Kuwaiti military and security forces.

- *An Iranian War of Intimidation in the Gulf or Gulf of Oman:* Iran does not have the air of sea power to win a naval war in the Gulf, or the amphibious and air assault capability to successfully invade even a small Southern Gulf state like Bahrain. Iran has, however, steadily built up its land and sea-based anti-ship missile capabilities, its air defenses along its southern Gulf coast, the strength of the naval branch of the Revolutionary Guards, its mine warfare capability, and its forces on the islands in the Gulf. It has acquired submarines and can use dhows and other small craft to infiltrate and attack naval and coastal targets. The US, British, and Southern Gulf navies can defeat any regular Iranian naval attack, but these steadily growing Iranian capabilities could be used for less orthodox military purposes, including threats and intimidation, and low-level and unconventional warfare. US forces would find it difficult to patrol the entire Gulf, and maintain the security of Gulf shipping, coastal, and off-shore facilities against such campaigns because of the sheer area to be covered and the unpredictable nature of Iranian actions. The US also cannot produce instant solutions to Iranian attacks. It will take time to prepare for and defeat well-organized Iranian uses of seapower, and the US military cannot guarantee that Iran will not provoke a series of crises or incidents that will lead to temporary success or incidents which temporarily affect the flow of Gulf shipping.
- *Mine Warfare in the Gulf:* Both Iran and Iraq have modern mines which are hard to detect and destroy. Both have large stocks of older mines that can be covertly deployed in the Gulf, or allowed to float in shipping lanes. The US is improving its mine warfare capabilities and has deployed some new mine warfare vessels in the Gulf. Broad coverage of the Gulf, however, requires strong local Southern Gulf mine warfare and maritime surveillance capabilities.
- *Air, missile, and coastal defense against sudden selective raids on critical targets:* The US cannot possibly provide comprehensive defense along a coastal area of more than 1,500 kilometers, or day-to-day coverage of the Gulf. There are many critical ports, oil and gas facilities, desalination plants, power plants, and other facilities that Iran or Iraq could attack successfully in slash and run raids before US forces could respond. Overall air and missile defense capability and maritime and coastal surveillance must be a Southern Gulf responsibility.
- *Divisions among the Southern Gulf States:* The US cannot resolve feuds, tensions, and local conflicts between the Southern Gulf states. It can attempt to mediate or negotiate, but US forces are not a substitute for cooperation and unity within the Southern Gulf, and can-

not deal with local quarrels that could divide the Southern Gulf, or lead given states to align themselves with Iran or Iraq.

- *Internal Unrest within a Southern Gulf State:* The US cannot use military force to save a regime from its own mistakes or its own people. Political unrest, extremism, internal violence, and coup attempts could bring a radical regime to power in the Southern Gulf, and change the regional alignments with Iran or Iraq. The US is a non-Arab and non-Islamic power and cannot use force to interfere in Southern Gulf internal issues. Similarly, US naval and air surveillance cannot substitute for local defense and internal security capabilities in preventing Iran or Iraq from smuggling in support to local dissidents.
- *Terrorism and Unconventional Warfare:* Terrorism and unconventional warfare can range from attacks on US forces designed to create domestic political problems in the US to the use of weapons of mass destruction against major targets in the Southern Gulf. The US can assist in dealing with such threats, but defense against this kind of low-level or covert threat requires the coverage of the entire Southern Gulf, and must be primarily dependent on local internal security capabilities.
- *Use of Weapons of Mass Destruction:* As is discussed later in this analysis, the stakes change fundamentally if Iran and/or Iraq are willing to use weapons of mass destruction or even threaten the use of such weapons. The US now has far stronger conventional capabilities than capabilities to conduct wars which involve the actual or threatened use of chemical, biological, and nuclear weapons. The US needs to develop much stronger counterproliferation capabilities if it is to deal with such threats, and Southern Gulf countries need to develop the kind of air and missile defenses, and nuclear-biological-chemical (NBC) war fighting capabilities, necessary to give them the resolve, deterrent, and defense capabilities they need to deal with Iranian and Iraqi weapons of mass destruction.

Many of these uncertainties are more an indication of the fact that the Southern Gulf must be ready to play a strong role in its own defense than an indication of US weakness or vulnerability. The United States alone cannot hope to fill a power vacuum in the Southern Gulf. As is the case in NATO, the defense of the Southern Gulf must be a collective responsibility and even the smallest Gulf nations must play a vital role.

6

New Arrangements
with Regional Powers

Fortunately, the US has made major progress in evolving new relationships with a number of its Gulf allies which improve its regional presence, power projection capabilities, sustainability, and interoperability with allied forces—although it still faces major limitations in terms of the rapid deployment of heavy land forces. The US has concluded or strengthened bilateral defense cooperation agreements with almost all friendly states in the Gulf since Desert Storm. The US has obtained agreements to deploy storage sites for USAF bare base sets (Harvest Falcon), US Navy forward logistic sets, water and fuel distribution equipment, medical supplies and infrastructure, support vehicles and equipment, and rations.

These agreements frame new bilateral relationships and include provisions for access/use of facilities, prepositioning of equipment, status of US personnel, and host-nation support. They strengthen coalition deterrence, provide greater strategic flexibility, more rapid responses to crises, and facilitate the transition to a wartime posture. They are also essential to any effective US deployment to a region that is 7,000 air miles and 8,000 sea miles from the US.[83] The US has also sold large amounts of military equipment to key Gulf allies that improve their military capabilities and the contribution they can make to any coalition in a future Gulf War.

The key arrangements the US has reached with powers in the region are summarized in Table Nine.

There are obvious uncertainties in such arrangements. The US is dealing with sovereign countries that will pursue their own strategic interests in a crisis. It is also dealing with nations which often have deep internal divisions which limit the level of cooperation they can implement with the US. Bahrain and Saudi Arabia show growing signs of internal instability, and Southern Gulf states must be sensitive to the political backlash from US ties to Israel and the pressures of Arab nationalism and Islamic fundamentalism. Most Southern Gulf states disagree

TABLE NINE   Support to the US from Southern Gulf States

Bahrain:

- Bahrain has maintained close military relations with the US since Britain departed the Gulf. On December 31, 1971, the US and Bahrain signed a leasing agreement allowing the US to use 10 acres at Jufair to support its Middle East Force (MEF) in the Gulf—this included US use of a transmitter and antennae, priority use of Berth 1 at the port, waterfront ship repair facilities, and land rights, and hangar and office space at Muharraq Airfield.[84]
- As a result of the tensions following the October War, Bahrain officially terminated this arrangement on October 20, 1973, but this termination had no practical effect, and Bahrain quietly reinstated the lease in July 1975—expanding its scope on August 12, 1975, and June 30, 1977. The agreement of June 30, 1977, is typical of many aspects of the informal cooperation between the US and Gulf states before the Gulf War. Officially, the US Navy no longer homeported the MEF in Bahrain, but maintained a "temporary duty administrative unit." In practice, the US continued to "homeport" its Gulf naval forces (Middle East Force) in Manama and use the port facility at Mina Al-Sulman.[85]
- Bahrain provided extensive support, basing, and repair support to the US during "Operation Earnest Will" in the tanker war with Iran in 1987–1988. This US operation required extensive support from friendly Gulf states. The US used a total of 27 warships, which conducted 127 missions from July, 1987 to December 1988. Bahrain played a critical role in helping the US recover the USS Stark after it hit a mine in the Gulf, and also supported the US during Operation Praying Mantis—when the US attacked Iranian oil platforms in the Gulf.
- Bahrain furnished extensive naval and air facilities to the US and Britain during the Gulf War. In September, 1990, Bahrain accepted US F/A-18, A-6, EA-6 and AV-8B air units, and British Tornado units. Bahrain provided a 200-man infantry company to Joint Forces Command (East). Bahrain's air force was relatively new and just absorbed deliveries of F-16s. Nevertheless, the Bahrain Air Force flew a total of 266 combat sorties. It used its new F-16s to fly 166 defensive and offensive counter-air sorties, averaging 4–6 sorties per day. It used its F-5s to fly 122 interdiction sorties, averaging about 3–4 sorties per day. It attacked targets like radar sites, Silkworm sites, and artillery positions.[86]
- Bahrain deployed a squadron of fighter aircraft to Kuwait when Iraqi forces moved towards the Kuwaiti border in October 1994.[87]
- On October 22, 1991, Bahrain signed a ten year bilateral agreement, expanding the US military presence in Bahrain. The agreement expanded US prepositioning in Bahrain, called for expanded joint exercises and training, allowed the US to set up a JTME (USCENTCOM headquarters), and increased US access to Bahraini ports and airfields. The US now has several warehouses of prepositioned equipment and supplies at Sheik Isa Air Base.
- On July 1, 1995, Bahrain agreed to allow the US to create the headquarters for its new 5th Fleet in Bahrain, with an Admiral and a headquarters contingent.

(continues)

TABLE NINE   (*continued*)

This headquarters commands a force that now averages 15 vessels, including a carrier. There are now roughly 1,500 US military personnel based in Bahrain. The fleet is now officially based at Mina Sulman.

- In November 1995, Bahrain agreed to allow the US to temporarily deploy 18 additional US combat aircraft in Bahrain to make up for the "gap" created by the need to withdraw a US carrier from the Gulf before a new one could be deployed.[88]
- Joint exercises between Bahraini and US forces have increased from two per year after the Gulf War to nearly eight.
- There is a US Office of Military Cooperation in Bahrain with six military officers, and one civilian.
- Bahrain purchases large amounts of US military equipment. Between FY1950 and FY1990, it purchased $874.8 million worth of US Foreign Military Sales (FMS), and took delivery on $545.2 million worth.[89] Since the Gulf War, it has purchased $197.9 million worth of US Foreign Military Sales (FMS), and taken delivery on $239.6 million worth.[90] Bahrain also receives about $200,000–$400,000 a year worth of IMET military training assistance from the US.[91]

Kuwait:

- Until the tanker war of 1987–1988, Kuwait attempted to maintain its security by balancing the competing political and military interests of its neighbors in ways where it could obtain support from a wide range of countries and defuse potential threats through financial aid or political accommodation. Kuwait then obtained the reflagging of its tankers from the US during the tanker war, cooperated closely with the US to ensure its security against Iran, and bought US F/A-18 aircraft to modernize its air force.
- The US and Kuwait cooperated closely after Iraq's invasion of Kuwait, and Kuwait provided the US with $16.056 billion in direct aid during the Gulf War, and $44 million in goods and services, for a total of $16.059 billion.[92] The US played a key role in helping Kuwait to rebuild its military forces before the liberation of Kuwait, and this help enabled Kuwait to deploy some 7,000 troops and 60 tanks as part of the Saudi-led Joint Force Command (East).[93]
- Less than 200 trained Kuwaiti Air Force personnel were in service at the start of Desert Storm, but Kuwait used French Air Force and US contract personnel to support its 15 operational Mirage F-1s, and 19 A-4s. The Kuwaiti Air Force also had 12 armed helicopters. Kuwaiti units flew 568 interdiction missions and 212 battlefield interdiction missions for a total of 780 sorties. About 650 of these sorties were A-4 sorties, and Kuwaiti A-4s flew an average of about 18–20 sorties per day. Kuwaiti Mirage F-1s flew the remaining 130 sorties, flying 4 to 10 sorties per day. Operational availability rates averaged 80–85% per day. Kuwait lost one A-4 on the first day of fighting, but attacked Iraqi artillery and infantry locations, and some Iraqi air defense positions throughout the war.

(*continues*)

TABLE NINE   (*continued*)

- The US Fifth Special Forces trained some 6,300 Kuwaitis for the Free Kuwait Forces, and the US Navy Special Forces Command trained 224 Kuwait marines and sailors.
- Since the Iraqi invasion of Kuwait, Kuwait has signed security agreements with Britain, France, Russia, and the US. Kuwait signed a 10 year bilateral agreement with the US on September 19, 1991. This agreement provided for $35 million per year in Kuwaiti payments to offset the cost of US military support.[94]
- Kuwait now relies heavily on the US to help it in rebuilding and expanding its military forces, and its military facilities are being sized and redesigned to support the rapid deployment, support, and sustainment of US land and air units. A US-Kuwait Defense Review Group helps coordinate these efforts.
- Kuwait is equipping much of its force structure with US Army and US aircraft, and has bought 40 F/A-18s and M-1A2 tanks, M-2/M-3 armored fighting vehicles, and US artillery, and Kuwait has support contracts with US defense contractors that provide it with increased sustainability as well as increased capability to support the deployment of US forces. Between FY1950 and FY1990, Kuwait purchased $3,541.5 million worth of US Foreign Military Sales (FMS), and took delivery on $1,089.0 million worth.[95] Since the Gulf War, it has purchased $3,495.8 million worth of US Foreign Military Sales (FMS), and taken delivery on $1,721.6 million worth.[96] The US has an Office of Military Cooperation in Kuwait, with a Brigadier General, eleven military personnel, two civilians, and one local employee.
- Kuwait supports the US in maintaining USAF combat aircraft on Kuwaiti soil—including 24 USAF A-10 attack aircraft based at Ahmed Al-Jaber air base. It is creating a new air base in southern Kuwait to facilitate rapid US air deployments in the most defensible part of Kuwaiti air space.[97] Kuwait has bought $145.6 million worth of US military construction services since the Gulf War.[98]
- Kuwait allows a cadre of US Army personnel to be stationed in Kuwait, and is paying $215 million to finance the prepositioning of the combat equipment of one US Army mechanized brigade (three armored companies and three mechanized companies)—including 58 M-1A2 tanks, M-2A2 Bradleys, and M-109A6 Paladin artillery weapons. A company of US Army military police provides security for the equipment and 600 employees of the DynCorp are responsible for its maintenance.
- The Kuwaiti C⁴I system is now interoperable with that of US forces. The C⁴I links for the US-operated Patriot units in Kuwait are linked to those for Patriot units in Saudi Arabia and to US satellite warning systems that detect the nature and vector of missile launches.
- Kuwaiti land, air, and naval forces now conduct extensive combined training with the US. Kuwait and the US held at least eight major exercises between November 1991 and January 1995, including "Eager Mace," "Intrinsic Action," and "Native Fury." These exercises include practicing the unloading of

---

(*continues*)

72

tanks from prepositioning ships and the defense of Kuwait City from an Iraqi invasion.

- Kuwait and the US conducted Operation Vigilant Warrior in early October, 1994, in response to the build-up of 70,000–80,000 Iraqi troops, 1,100 tanks, 1,000 AFVs, and 700 artillery pieces in the border area. Kuwait provided major offset aid, air and kind, and facility support as the US began supplementing the 13,000 troops already deployed in Kuwait with the 1st Marine Expeditionary Force, 24th Infantry Division, and added Patriot forces.

Oman:

- The US has cooperated with Oman since the time of the Dhofar Rebellion and the US provided informal assistance to Oman, Britain, and Iran during their campaigns against the Dhofar rebels. The US supported Oman in its long confrontation with the PDRY, and in dealing with the potential threat posed by Iran after the beginning of the Iran-Iraq War. Oman has long permitted US-CENTCOM to conduct exercises in Oman, and US Navy ships to use Omani facilities. Oman has provided data on tanker and other ship transits of the Straits of Hormuz to the US and UK from its base on Goat Island since the early 1980s.
- Oman and the US signed a military access agreement in July 1981, which provided US access to building cantonments, hardened shelters, warehouses, and other facilities at Seeb, Masirah, Khasab, and Thumrait air bases, and ports at Muscat and Salalah, in return for $320 million in US funds to build-up these facilities.[99] The US provided over $199.1 million in FMS credits to Oman between FY1980 and FY1990, and about $853,000 in IMET assistance. During FY1981–FY1985, the US provided support to Oman for the construction of four air bases at Masirah, Seeb, Khasab, and Thumrait that could be used by US air units in rapid deployment to the Gulf.
- This construction included facilities for rear-area staging and forward deployment, and included improved operations, personnel, storage, and maintenance facilities. The US Navy developed an aircraft maintenance facility, ground support equipment shop, warehouse facility, and ammunition storage facility. The US Army created a staging base at Masirah to support the forward deployment of US Army forces. The US helped provide hardened shelters, dispersal and access pavements, environmentally controlled warehouses, transient billeting, and cantonment support areas at Seeb and Thumrait. The US access agreement is reviewed every five years, and the latest review was due in 1995.
- Oman allowed the US and Britain to use Oman as a staging base and to deploy reconnaissance aircraft during the tanker war, and Gulf Wars, and allowed the US to stage reconnaissance and air-control flights out of Oman during Operation Praying Mantis—when the US attacked Iranian oil platforms in the Gulf. Oman provided about 950 troops to the Arab Joint Forces Command (East) during the Gulf War.

(*continues*)

TABLE NINE   *(continued)*

- Oman has regularly renewed its 1981 access agreement with the US. Oman deployed a squadron of fighter aircraft to Kuwait when Iraqi forces moved towards the Kuwaiti border in October 1994.[100] Many of Oman's arms are British-supplied, and Oman lacks the funds to make major military purchases. Oman did, however, purchase $163.3 million worth of US Foreign Military Sales (FMS) between FY1950 and FY1990, and took delivery on $91.8 million worth.[101]
- Since the Gulf War, it has purchased $13.2 million worth of US Foreign Military Sales (FMS), and taken delivery on $56.6 million worth.[102] Oman also receives about $110,000 a year worth of IMET military training assistance from the US, that trains about 16 Omani officers per year. A total of 80 Omani personnel were trained as part of the IMET program during 1990–1994.[103] The US maintains an Office of Military Cooperation in Oman, with five military, one civilian, and one local employee.
- Oman works closely with Britain, and there are roughly 200 British soldiers training the Omani Army. There are British officers and NCOs seconded to the Omani Navy, and some 80 British officers seconded to the Omani air force. British SAS personnel have trained the Omani anti-terrorist force and assist in surveillance of the border with Yemen. France provides a limited amount of training for Omani officers.

Qatar:

- The US did not begin to develop security arrangements with Qatar until the tanker war of 1987–1988, and only began to develop close security arrangements during the Gulf War. Considerable tension existed over Qatar's purchase of smuggled Stinger missiles from Afghanistan during March 1988 to November 1990. Since that time, however, relations have steadily improved.
- Qatar permitted US air units to stage out of Qatar during the Gulf War. Qatar provided a 1,600-man mechanized battalion with 25 tanks, 60 other armored vehicles, and 3–5 artillery weapons. This force fought well at the Battle of Khafji, and in Joint Forces Command (East). Qatar also committed 700 men, 21 fighters, and 12 armed helicopters from its small air force. Qatari Mirage F-1s flew 41 interdiction sorties, with a maximum of about 5 sorties per day. Qatari Alphajets flew two sorties. The Qatari Air Force was forced to cancel or abort 22 sorties, but 16 of these cancellations were due to weather.[104]
- On June 22, 1992, Qatar negotiated a bilateral security arrangement with the US that offers the US access to Qatari air and naval facilities. Since that time Qatar has conducted an increasing number of exercises with US forces.
- In March 1995, Qatar formally agreed to the prepositioning of the heavy equipment for one US Army mechanized brigade in Qatar—including up to 110 US M-1A2 tanks. Warehouses are now under construction in Doha to preposition US equipment The Qatari air force has also begun to conduct combined air exercises with the US, and may acquire a site in Qatar.[105]

(continues)

TABLE NINE   *(continued)*

- Qatari forces are largely French-equipped and only have limited interoperability and sustainability with US forces. Qatar only purchased $1.9 million worth of US Foreign Military Sales (FMS) between FY1950 and FY1990, and took delivery on $1.9 million worth.[106] A US Military Liaison Office opened in Doha in 1991. Since the Gulf War, Qatar has purchased $2.7 million worth of US Foreign Military Sales (FMS), and taken delivery on $1.4 million worth.[107]

Saudi Arabia:

- Although the US does not have a formal status of forces agreement with Saudi Arabia, it has long had close military ties to Saudi Arabia. The US first leased port and air base facilities in Dhahran, Saudi Arabia, in 1943. It renewed these leases on April 22, 1957 and maintained them until April 2, 1962—when they were canceled both for political reasons and because the US Strategic Air Command ceased to forward deploy the B-47. Saudi Arabia renewed its US Military Training Mission Agreement with the US in June 1992.[108]
- During the late 1970s and 1980s, Saudi Arabia increased the size of its air bases and port facilities to aid in US power projection to Saudi Arabia, and created massive stockpiles of munitions and equipment, and support facilities, that could be used by US forces deploying to Saudi Arabia. Saudi Arabia purchased $16 billion worth of US military construction services during this period, and supervised military construction worth billions of dollars more.[109]
- The US and Saudi Arabia cooperated closely in setting up combined air and naval defenses against Iran beginning in 1983, when Iraq came under serious military pressure from Iran. The two countries conducted combined exercises, and cooperated in establishing the "Fahd Line," which created an Air Defense Identification Zone and forward air defense system off the Saudi coast. This cooperation helped Saudi Arabia defend its air space and shoot down an Iranian F-4 which tested Saudi defenses on June 5, 1984. The US and Saudi Arabia have jointly operated E-3A AWACS units in Saudi Arabia ever since. The US and Saudi Arabia also cooperated closely during the tanker war of 1987–1988.
- The US deployed massive land and air units to Saudi Arabia during the Gulf War, and jointly commanded UN Coalition forces with Saudi Arabia during Desert Storm. Saudi forces played a major role in the air and land campaigns. Saudi Arabia also provided the US with $12.809 billion in direct aid during the Gulf War, and $4.045 billion in goods and services, for a total of $16.854 billion.[110]
- Saudi Arabia commanded both Arab task forces—Joint Forces Command (East) and Joint Forces Command (North).[111] Saudi forces were organized under the command of Lt. General Prince Khalid Bin Sultan al-Saud. The Arab task forces reported to Prince Khalid through a Joint Forces Command in the Saudi Ministry of Defense, and were divided into a Joint Forces Command (North), a Joint Forces Command (East), and a Joint Forward Forces Command Ar'Ar (the command of the Arab defensive forces screening the border area). The Ar'Ar

(continues)

TABLE NINE   (*continued*)

command was subordinated to the Joint Forces Command (North). It included two Saudi National Guard battalions, a Saudi Army airborne battalion, and a Pakistani armored brigade with about 5,500 men, over 100 tanks, and about 90 other additional armored vehicles and artillery weapons. These forces did not play an offensive role in Desert Storm.[112] By the time the AirLand phase of the war began, the Saudi ground forces in the theater totaled nearly 50,000 men, with about 270 main battle tanks, 930 other armored fighting vehicles, 115 artillery weapons, and over 400 anti-tank weapons.[113]

- The Saudi Air Force flew a total of 6,852 sorties between January 17, 1991 and February 28—ranking second after the US in total air activity during the Gulf War, and flying about 6% of all sorties flown. These sorties included 1,133 interdiction missions, and 523 battlefield air interdiction missions, for a total of 1,656 offensive missions. The RSAF flew 2,050 defensive counter-air missions, 129 offensive counter-air missions, and 102 escort missions for a total of 2,281 air defense sorties. The RSAF flew 118 reconnaissance sorties, 85 E3-A AWACS sorties, 485 refueling sorties, and 1,829 airlift sorties.[114] During the slightly longer period of January 16 to February 28, Saudi Air Force F-15C units flew 2,088 sorties (over one-third the total F-15C sorties flown by the USAF) and 451 Tornado ADV sorties. Saudi pilots were as capable in these air defense sorties as most pilots in NATO. The RSAF also flew 665 Tornado GR1/IDS strike sorties, 1,129 F-5 sorties, and 118 RF-5 sorties. Saudi F-15Cs shot down three Iraqi Mirage F-1s with air-to-air missiles—including the only double kill by a single fighter in the war on January 24, 1991. The RSAF lost only two aircraft—one Tornado GR1 to anti-aircraft fire and one F-5 to unknown causes.[115]

- Since the Gulf War, the US has expanded its security arrangements with Saudi Arabia. Although no formal status of forces agreements exist, the US and Saudi Arabia have expanded the USMTM agreement to increase US access to Saudi air and seaports, including Jubail, and have improved the capabilities of the combined AWACS force. The US deploys a wing of aircraft in southern Saudi Arabia, including F-117 and U-2 aircraft. Saudi Arabia has increased stocks of selected spares and electronics to support US forces in deploying—including enough parts and supplies to support 15 USAF tactical fighter equivalents—and has increased the number of combined exercises with US forces.[116] It is standardizing key aspects of its C4I system to make them interoperable with US C⁴I systems, including theater missile defense arrangements for Saudi Arabia's Patriot missiles. Saudi Arabia has provided the US with additional facilities, and has ordered $1.6 billion worth of US military construction services since the Gulf War—$610,8 million of which has been delivered.[117]

- Saudi Arabia has long been one of the largest single customers for US military exports—and Saudi purchases have both increased interoperability and sustainability with US forces, and have reduced the unit cost of equipment purchased by US forces. Between FY1950 and FY1990, Saudi Arabia purchased $35,876.0 million worth of US Foreign Military Sales (FMS), and took delivery

(*continues*)

TABLE NINE *(continued)*

on $23,799.4 million worth.[118] Since the Gulf War, it has purchased $24,835.5 million worth of US Foreign Military Sales (FMS), and taken delivery on $8,818 million worth.[119]

- Since the Gulf War, Saudi Arabia has made major purchases of US M-1 tanks, M-2/M-3 armored vehicles, and US artillery and related support systems which increase both Saudi interoperability with US forces and Saudi capability to support the rapid deployment of heavy US ground forces to Saudi Arabia. Although Saudi Arabia has not agreed to formal prepositioning of US Army combat unit equipment in Saudi Arabia, it has carried out combined exercises with US land forces since 1991, and is considering storage of selected US Army heavy combat equipment. The US maintains a US Military Training Mission in Saudi Arabia with 69 military four civilians, and nine local personnel.
- The Saudi National Guard has long relied largely on US equipment, and on training support by the US Vinnell Corporation.

United Arab Emirates:

- The US did not begin to develop close security arrangements with the UAE until the tanker war of 1987–1988, but the US and UAE cooperated closely during both the tanker war and Gulf War. The UAE provided port call facilities and support during Operation Earnest Will. The US Navy and MEF conducted a combined exercise with UAE in July 1990, after Saddam Hussein began to threaten the UAE.
- The UAE provided the US with $6.572 billion in direct aid during the Gulf War, and $218 million in goods and services, for a total of $6.455 billion.[120] The UAE committed a Motorized Infantry Battalion to Joint Forces Command (East) and created a combined aviation battalion with Kuwait. It used its 7,000-man air force to fly 109 sorties, including 58 Mirage 2000 interdiction sorties, 45 C-212 and C-130 airlift sorties, and six Mirage 2000 reconnaissance sorties. The UAE Air Force had reasonable readiness. It canceled or aborted 18 sorties, but only two due to maintenance reasons. Its Mirage 2000 fighters attacked targets like Iraqi infantry and mechanized forces, artillery positions, and supply areas.[121]
- The UAE negotiated a security arrangement with the US in 1992 that offered the US access to UAE air and naval facilities. The UAE and US signed a Defense Cooperation Agreement on July 23, 1994.
- A small amount of US Navy equipment is prepositioned at Jebel Ali and a small US Navy support facility exists in Fujirah. US Navy ships make regular port calls to the UAE—Jebel Ali is one of the most frequent port calls in the world for the US Navy. Fujirah, on the Gulf of Oman, also allows the US to provide logistic support to reach destinations in the Gulf without going through the Straits of Hormuz by moving from ports in Fujirah along a modern highway to locations in the Southern Gulf.

(continues)

TABLE NINE   (*continued*)

- In 1995, the UAE agreed to host a US Army prepositioned brigade with 120 tanks and 70 AIFVs. An agreement in principle has already been signed and negotiations are underway over cost-sharing.
- UAE forces have conducted combined air exercises with the US. The UAE deployed a squadron of fighter aircraft to Kuwait when Iraqi forces moved towards the Kuwaiti border in October 1994.[122]
- UAE forces have increasing amounts of US equipment, including IHawk missiles and AH-64 attack helicopters. Between FY1950 and FY1990, the UAE purchased $1,048.8 million worth of US Foreign Military Sales (FMS), and took delivery on $313.2 million worth.[123] Since the Gulf War, it has purchased $592.5 million worth of US Foreign Military Sales (FMS), and taken delivery on $586.6 million worth.[124] UAE forces are, however, equipped with weapons from a wide range of sources, and only have moderate interoperability and sustainability with US forces. The US has a military liaison office in the UAE with six military, one civilian, and two local personnel to manage military programs in the country.

---

with the US effort to try to isolate Iran, and many feel the time has come to ease sanctions on Iraq. The Southern Gulf states all face major cash flow crises which are limiting the force expansion and military modernization, and they have shown little progress in moving away from strategic dependence on the US, in creating effective regional cooperation under the Gulf Cooperation Council, or in reforming their economies in ways which will ease their long-term problems in funding military expenditures and arms imports. There are significant uncertainties in how long the US can preserve the present level of strategic cooperation in the face of internal divisions within the Gulf states, and economic pressures that are leading many Gulf states to limit their military spending and burden sharing expenditures.

At the same time, these arrangements have helped to allow the US to substantially increase its presence in the Gulf, to include SOF and Patriot units, limited land-based air forces under Operation Southern Watch, and a near continuous carrier battle group and marine amphibious ready group presence in the region. The US has also been able to increase its number of combined exercises, military construction, and security assistance. The US now carries out roughly 100 joint and combined exercises in the Middle East each year. These exercises include numerous naval and special operations exercises, the Intrinsic Action series in Kuwait, and the Ultimate Resolve series of exercises. These exercises are used to maintain access, promote interoperability with regional partners, enhance the forward presence of US forces, and improve the individual and collective capabilities of the GCC states.

The importance of these improvements in prepositioning and cooperation in the region became clear in October 1994, when Iraq moved two
Republican Guards divisions and three additional divisions to positions
near its border with Kuwait. The US had to rush in additional forces to
the Gulf, beginning on October 9, to supplement the 13,000 US personnel
already in the theater. These forces initially included the 18,000 men in
the 1st Marine Expeditionary Force, 16,000 troops from the US Army's
24th Infantry Division, 306 fixed wing aircraft (including A-10s, F-16s,
RF-4Cs, F-15Es, F-15Cs, F-111s, EF-111s, F-117s, JSTARS, F/A-18s, B-52s,
and E-3As, 58 helicopters (including 54 AH-64s), two batteries of Patriot
missiles, and a carrier battle group. The US then decided to deploy
another 73 fixed wing aircraft.

By October 12, the US had a total of 19,241 men in the Gulf area (1,923
Army, 11,171 Navy, 1,977 Marine, 3,844 Air Force, 173 Special Operations,
and 153 Joint Task Force Headquarters). It had two carrier task forces
with 15 ships (counting one carrier battle group in the Red Sea), and 200
combat aircraft. It was deploying significant numbers of aircraft, US
Army units were beginning to join the prepositioned US armor in
Kuwait, and 5 Marine Corps Maritime Prepositioning Ships, 8 US Army
Brigade Afloat Ships, and 6 USAF and US Army Prepositioning Ships
were moving towards the Gulf. US forces were involved in combined
exercises with Kuwaiti forces in the border area within a matter of days,
and the US held a major, demonstrative, anti-armor exercise using B-52-
strike aircraft by the end of October. In contrast, the Gulf Cooperation
Council was only able to make a token commitment of the Peninsula
Shield force—a force which lacked the combat capability to play any significant role in defending Kuwait.

While Iraq soon backed down, and the US was able to cut its planned
deployments, at one point the US had 210,000 personnel deployed, en
route, or on alert. This total is summarized in Table Ten, and include personnel from all four armed services. It also provides a good example of
the forces the US would have to deploy to deter a major regional contingency in the Gulf.

The US demonstrated a similar mix of resolve and capabilities in late
August, 1995, when there were indications that Iraq might again be
deploying forces to invade Kuwait. It deployed a total of 12 prepositioning ships from Diego Garcia and other locations to the Gulf, with enough
armor, artillery, food, fuel, water, vehicles, and other equipment to sustain a 16,500 Marine Corps MEF (Forward), and a 15,000–17,000 man US
Army Corps in combat.[125]

It demonstrated its resolve and capabilities again in January 1996,
when US intelligence concluded that Iraq had brought five armored
divisions to sufficient readiness to deploy to Kuwait with only five

TABLE TEN   US Deployments to the Gulf Region on October 11, 1994

Location	Ground Forces	Ships	Aircraft
In region	3,600	15	200
Deploying	36,100	21	467
On Alert	155,000	0	196
Total	194,000	33	863

Source: Steven R. Bowman, "Military Deployments to the Gulf Region," Congressional Research Service, CRS 94-790F, Washington, DC, October 12, 1994.

hours notice. The US deployed 12 prepositioning ships—enough to equip a Marine Division and a US Army Brigade—into the Gulf. The US did not send troops, but this move allowed the US to deploy up to 20,000 troops on short notice. The US also deployed additional combat aircraft to Bahrain and Kuwait, and extended a joint exercise with Kuwait. The US already had some 20,000 troops in the Middle East area, and deployed 35 ships, and 14,000 sailors and US Marines, in its Fifth Fleet between the Suez Canal and Indian Ocean. These forces included the Nimitz carrier battle group, and a Marine Corps amphibious ready group. It is interesting to note that the US only had 250 naval personnel stationed permanently ashore in Bahrain.[126] It also demonstrated its resolve in September 1996, by responding to Saddam Hussein's attacks on his Kurds by launching cruise missile attacks, expanding the "no fly" zone in Southern Iraq, and deploying added troops, aircraft, and ships to the Gulf.

The key problem that the US now faces in improving its cooperative arrangements with its Gulf allies is to complete the prepositioning of US Army, Marine Corps, and air equipment to the Gulf. The US feels this prepositioning is essential to improve the speed of US deployment capability, and to provide the ability to deter or halt any sudden Iraqi move against Kuwait. Its goal is to have enough prepositioning and forward basing capability by 2000 to deploy 8–10 tactical air wing equivalents within five days, and at least two US Army divisions within two weeks. These forces would be followed by a 4–5 division US Army Corps, a Marine Expeditionary Force, and supporting air wings within eight weeks—twice as fast as it took to deploy a similar force in 1991.[127]

So far, the US has prepositioned one mechanized brigade set into Kuwait. This brigade set is located in northern Kuwait, and was activated in October, 1994. The US was able to fly in troops, marry them up with their prepositioned equipment, and deploy the brigade to the Kuwaiti border within two weeks.[128] The US has prepositioned most of one brigade set afloat, and is seeking the additional sealift necessary to preposition two armored and two mechanized battalions on five new RO-RO ships in the Gulf.[129]

The Marine Corps Maritime Prepositioning Force now includes three Maritime Prepositioning Squadrons, each able to support a Marine Expeditionary Force (Forward) and nearly 15,000 men for 30 days with equipment and supplies. One of these squadrons is normally deployed at Diego Garcia. The Air Force has four logistic ships, carrying supplies and ammunition, and the US Army now has two container ships which carry 30 days of supplies for the early deploying units of the entire contingency Corps.[130] The US goal is to have about 200,000 tons of heavy weapons, support equipment, and other supplies afloat in the region, and another 350,000 tons prepositioned ashore.[131]

The US has negotiated with Oman, Qatar, Saudi Arabia, and the UAE over the prepositioning of a second and third set on land. Saudi Arabia is the ideal location for such a set, but has resisted these efforts because of its fear that such a high profile action could increase its problems with Islamic extremists. The prepositioning of a brigade set offers the US major advantages in terms of time and cost. A brigade can deploy to a prepositioned brigade set in six days at a cost of $26 million. It would take the equivalent of 28 Boeing 747 aircraft to move the soldiers and 28 C-141 flights to bring in additional equipment. In contrast, such a redeployment would cost $345 million, would take 28 days to airlift an entire brigade, and would require 679 C-141 flights and 532 C-5 flights.[132]

In addition to improving its land warfare capabilities, the US must complete arrangements with the Southern Gulf states to improve its ability to rapidly base, sustain, and control over 800 combat aircraft, and to support and sustain a Corps over an extended period of time. The US must also support and modernize prepositioning for the Air Force and US Marine Corps.

Deploying and sustaining such a force requires major improvements in afloat prepositioning, rail equipment, prepositioning over 1,000 rail cars for heavy/oversized cargoes, and buying additional containers and loading equipment and a new containerized ammunition facility on the West Coast. It requires new or improved training layberths, raid and airheads, deployment training centers, port facilities, and movement control automation. It also requires the US to raise its number of surge medium-speed roll-on/roll-off sealift ships from 8 to 19, its number of slower roll-on-roll-off ships from 26 to 28, and full support of an existing force of 12 US Army equipment afloat ships.[133]

It is also important to note that the Gulf states are not the only aspect of regional strategic cooperation. The Bright Star series of exercises in Egypt involve massive combined exercises between US and Egyptian forces. The November 1995 series of exercises, for example, directly involved more than 5,000 troops, and included forces from Britain, France, and the UAE. The total forces involved in some form of training involved some 33,000 Egyptian troops and 22,000 US troops. The exercise phase involved 500 British troops, 500 French troops, and 200 from the UAE. It involved some 2,700 sorties by over 700 aircraft, and exercises by more than 100 tanks and a carrier battle group.[134] Egypt could play a major role in the Gulf in many contingencies if it had US support in the form of C^4I/BM capabilities, sustainability, and combat coordination.

Iran and Iraq can never entirely ignore the capabilities of Israel—particularly as advances in the peace process steadily cut the political liabilities that are likely to be triggered by Israeli intervention in a large-scale Gulf conflict. Further, Iran and Iraq must consider Israel's nuclear deterrent and the risks inherent in any Iranian and Iraqi action in the Gulf that threatened to expand outside the region. If Iran and Iraq are potential threats to Israel, the favor is more than returned in kind.

7

The Impact of US Military Aid and Arms Sales

The US has other tools that strengthen its contingency capabilities in the Southern Gulf. The US only makes limited use of economic or military aid as a tool for strengthening its contingency capabilities in the Gulf—in part because of the steady world-wide reductions the US is making in all forms of spending on aid. Such military aid is unnecessary in the case of the wealthier Gulf states—Kuwait, Qatar, Saudi Arabia, and the UAE. Bahrain and Oman, however, lack the funds to pay for the modernization of their military forces, and Oman has only received limited aid from the other Southern Gulf states.

The recent patterns in US aid to the Gulf are shown in Table Eleven, although they do not include the full value of surplus military equipment transfers. It is striking how little aid is given to any Gulf state, and how little is given to Bahrain and Oman in particular. In contrast, Egypt and Israel received over $5 billion a year, and a state like Yemen—which supported Iraq during the Gulf War—received a total of $19 million in aid in FY1993, $16.9 million in FY1994, and $12.4 million in FY1995. Even Djibouti received more aid than Bahrain and Oman combined in FY1993, FY1994, and FY1995.

Ideally, such aid to Bahrain and Oman should be provided by the other Southern Gulf states. In practice, though, it is becoming increasingly clear that Bahrain and Oman will not get the aid they need unless there are major shifts in the policies of their neighbors. Accordingly, there are good reasons to rethink the present patterns of US aid in the Southern Gulf, and to consider expanding the transfer of surplus equipment to Bahrain and Oman as a means of providing aid without affecting the US budget. There are equally good reasons to rethink cuts in aid the US had pledged to Oman, but failed to deliver because of Congressional cuts. Oman has strongly supported the US in power projection in the region, and received remarkably little in return—particularly when one examines the past level of aid to states like

TABLE ELEVEN   US Aid to the Gulf States: FY1993–FY1996 ($Current Millions)

Country	Dev. Asst.	ESF/P.C.	PL-480/I	PL-480/II	Peace Corps	FMF Grant/ Financing	IMET	Total
FY1993 Actual Obligations								
Bahrain	0	0	0	0	0	0.5	0.106	0.606
Oman	0	0	0	0	0	1.0	0.11	1.11
Total	0	0	0	0	0	1.5	0.216	1.716
Total Middle East & North Africa	—	—	—	—	—	—	—	5,604.7
FY1994 Estimated Obligations								
Bahrain	0	0	0	0	0	0	0.056	0.056
Oman	0	0	0	0	0	0	0.054	0.054
Total	0	0	0	0	0	0	0.11	0.11
Total Middle East & North Africa	—	—	—	—	—	3,109.0	3.098	5,518.7
FY1995 Administration Request								
Bahrain	0	0	0	0	0	0	0.075	0.075
Oman	0	0	0	0	0	0	0.11	0.11
Total	0	0	0	0	0	0	0.185	0.185
Total Middle East & North Africa	—	—	—	—	—	3,107.3	4.26	5,406.7
FY1996 Administration Request								
Bahrain	0	0	0	0	0	0	0.1	0.1
Oman	0	0	0	0	0	0	0.11	0.11
Total	0	0	0	0	0	0	0.21	0.21
Total Middle East & North Africa	—	—	—	—	—	3,130	4.56	—

Source: Clyde R. Mark, *Middle East and North Africa: US Aid FY1993, 1994, 1995,* CRS 94-274F, March 28, 1995, and US Department of State, *Congressional Presentation for Foreign Operations, FY1996,* US Department of State, Washington, February 1995.

Yemen. The US clearly needs to examine whether critical systems like US fighters and frigates could be transferred to Bahrain and Oman as excess defense articles.[135]

The Impact of US Arms Sales

In contrast to aid, the US has long relied on arms sales as a way of strengthening allied forces in the Gulf. US foreign military sales (FMS) to the USCENTCOM region have totaled about $110 billion since 1950, and totaled about $62 billion between 1985 and 1994.[136] The US has used such arms sales to strengthen its contingency capabilities, and those of its allies, and has also helped improve allied contingency capabilities by providing extensive contractor training and support efforts, and mobile training and technical assistance field teams. The US now deploys more than 680 training personnel in the region.

US Arms Sales at the Time of the Gulf War

The importance of such arms transfers was demonstrated during and immediately after the Gulf War. The US strengthened Southern Gulf military capabilities by selling some $16.5 billion worth of FMS supplies during the crisis.[137] The US made major new deliveries of arms to Bahrain, Oman, Saudi Arabia, and the UAE to strengthen their forces by the time of Desert Storm. The US forces deploying to the Gulf were able to take advantage of many of the stocks of weapons and munitions, and the service facilities, the US had previously sold to key states like Saudi Arabia.[138] The major US orders and deliveries to the Southern Gulf states at the time of the Gulf War are summarized in Table Twelve.

US Arms Sales Since the Gulf War

The US has also reached major new sales agreements with the Southern Gulf states that have since allowed them to modernize their forces in ways that improve regional defense capabilities, substantially increase their interoperability with US forces, and increase their ability to support US deployments in the region. As Table Thirteen indicates, three critical southern Gulf states—Bahrain, Kuwait, and Saudi Arabia—have heavily standardized on US equipment since 1990. This standardization is particularly important, because Kuwait and Saudi Arabia are the key Gulf states that the US must include in a coalition which deals with a land threat from Iraq, and Bahrain, Kuwait, and Saudi Arabia are all critical to the rapid deployment of US air power.

TABLE TWELVE Major Deliveries and New Orders for US Military Equipment at the Time of the Gulf War (1 July 1990 to 30 September 1991)

Country	Deliveries			Orders		
	Item	Number	Value ($M)	Item	Number	Value ($M)
Bahrain	F-16C fighters	6	86.3	M577A2 command post	3	0.8
	UH-60L helicopters	1	6.5	M-113A3 APCs	28	9.7
	Maverick missiles	21	3.9	M-60A3 tanks	27	21.4
	TOW anti-tank missiles	200	2.3	M198 towed 155 mm	10	8.0
Oman	M-60A3 tanks	43	34.0	M-60A3 tanks	43	34.0
	TOW 2A missiles	425	5.0	TOW-2A	432	5.1
Saudi Arabia	F-15C fighters	22	592.4	F-15C fighters	20	545.5
	F-15D fighters	4	109.1	F-15D fighters	4	109.1
	UH-60 helicopter	13	94.4	UH-60 helicopter	8	64.8
	APC, full track	252	24.9	AH-64A helicopter	12	187.2
	Weapons carrier	86	18.8	River Patrol Boat	17	40.7
	M-60A3 tank	150	118.5	Light armored vehicles	1,317	1,492.5
	107 mm (4.2″) mortar	24	1.6	M-548A1 cargo carrier	50	3.3
	Maverick missiles	36	2.0	M-113A2 APC	207	15.2
	Sparrow missiles	700	99.4	M-113A2 command post	36	10.35
	Stinger missiles	150	11.6	M-577A3 command post	32	42.5
	TOW missiles	3,952	50.1	M-2A2 Bradley	200	359.2
				M-901A1 AT AFV	40	11.6
				M-60A3 tank	151	119.3
				M-1A2 tank	315	1,625.4

(continues)

TABLE TWELVE (continued)

Country	Deliveries			Orders		
	Item	Number	Value ($M)	Item	Number	Value ($M)
Saudi Arabia (cont.)				Phalanx CIWS	1	5.3
				MLRS	9	21.0
				Patriot missiles	300	221.4
				Sparrow AIM-7F	700	99.4
				Stinger missiles	150	8.4
				TOW 2 missiles	1,805	19.5
				TOW 2A missiles	1,740	19.6
				TOW 2A-3B missiles	591	6.9
UAE	Hawk missiles	40	9.8	Hawk missiles	40	9.8

Source: DSAA/COMP/PAID, November 28, 1994.

Table Thirteen also provides a much better picture of the military impact of US arms sales than data which simply report the dollar value of arms transfers. The total dollar value of US sales provides little indication of the changes in military capability that result from such sales. Such data also include a large amount of military construction, services, and maintenance related equipment. It is the number of weapons transferred that improves US power projection capabilities in terms of increased allied capabilities, interoperability, standardization, and sustainability.

These data are provided in Table Thirteen. Clearly, Southern Gulf states like Kuwait and Saudi Arabia have made important purchases of US armor, artillery, and aircraft, but the number of weapons involved scarcely reflects the massive arms build-up that some analysts have seen who have only looked at the total dollar value of post-Gulf War arms sales. In fact, post Gulf War transfers of key combat systems like tanks and supersonic fighter aircraft have been comparatively moderate, and scarcely out of proportion to the threat posed by Iran and Iraq.

TABLE THIRTEEN   FMS Orders of Major Combat Equipment for the Southern Gulf States: 1989–1994—Part One

Country	Tanks	APCs & AFVs	Artillery	AT Missiles	Aircraft			SAMs	Minor Surface Combat Ships	Anti-Ship Missiles
					Supersonic	Helicopters	Other			
Deliveries										
FY1989										
Saudi	—	33	—	52	—	—	—	—	—	—
UAE	—	—	—	—	—	—	—	49	—	—
FY1990										
Bahrain	—	—	—	—	12	—	—	—	—	—
Saudi	—	133	—	26	—	—	—	—	—	—
UAE	—	—	—	—	—	—	—	22	—	—
FY1991										
Bahrain	—	—	—	200	—	1	—	—	—	—
Oman	43	—	—	425	—	—	—	—	—	—
Saudi	150	207	24	3,592	26	13	15	150	—	—
UAE	—	—	—	—	—	—	—	140	—	—
FY1992										
Bahrain	27	102	—	—	—	—	—	—	—	—
Kuwait	—	—	—	—	20	—	—	—	—	—
Oman	—	—	—	5	—	—	—	—	—	—
Saudi	5	202	—	2,000	10	8	—	—	3	—

(*continues*)

TABLE THIRTEEN (continued)

Country	Tanks	APCs & AFVs	Artillery	AT Missiles	Aircraft			SAMs	Minor Surface Combat Ships	Anti-Ship Missiles
					Supersonic	Helicopters	Other			
FY1993										
Bahrain	—	12	10	3	—	—	—	54	—	—
Kuwait	—	—	—	—	20	—	—	—	—	42
Saudi	26	46	24	52	—	12	—	—	—	—
UAE	—	—	53	—	—	—	—	54	—	—
FY1994										
Kuwait	—	—	—	6	—	—	—	—	—	—
Saudi	—	75	1	6	—	—	—	—	—	—
UAE	—	—	—	—	—	—	—	12	—	—

Source: Adapted by the author from data provided by DSAA/COMP/PAID, November 28, 1994.

TABLE THIRTEEN   FMS Orders of Major Combat Equipment for the Southern Gulf States: 1989–1994—Part Two

Country	Tanks	APCs & AFVs	Artillery	AT Missiles	Aircraft Supersonic	Helicopters	Other	SAMs	Minor Surface Combat Ships	Anti-Ship Missiles
New Orders										
FY1989										
Bahrain	—	3	—	—	—	—	—	54	—	—
Saudi	—	200	—	1,016	—	—	—	—	—	—
FY1990										
Bahrain	—	98	—	—	—	1	—	—	—	—
Oman	43	—	—	—	—	—	—	—	—	—
Saudi	315	32	40	2,030	24	—	—	150	—	—
FY1991										
Bahrain	27	13	10	—	—	—	—	—	—	—
Kuwait	—	—	—	609	—	—	—	—	—	—
Saudi	151	1,610	28	4,136	—	—	20	300	17	—
UAE	—	—	—	—	—	—	—	40	—	—
FY1992										
Bahrain	—	2	—	—	—	—	—	—	—	—
Kuwait	—	—	—	711	—	—	—	—	—	—
UAE	—	—	—	—	—	20	—	—	—	—

(*continues*)

TABLE THIRTEEN *(continued)*

Country	Tanks	APCs & AFVs	Artillery	AT Missiles	Aircraft			SAMs	Minor Surface Combat Ships	Anti-Ship Missiles
					Supersonic	Helicopters	Other			
FY1993										
Bahrain	—	—	62	203	—	14	—	—	—	—
Kuwait	218	46	—	—	—	—	—	210	—	—
Saudi	—	—	—	—	72	—	—	661	—	—
FY1994										
Bahrain	—	—	—	102	—	—	—	—	—	—
UAE	—	—	—	—	—	10	—	—	—	—

Source: Adapted by the author from data provided by DSAA/COMP/PAID, November 28, 1994.

8

US Counterproliferation Capabilities

There is another aspect of US resources and capabilities that deserves special attention in dealing with future contingencies in the Gulf. Both Iran and Iraq have actively sought and acquired biological, chemical, and nuclear weapons. Both have obtained long-range missiles, and both used chemical weapons against each other in the Iran-Iraq War. While the UN victory in the Gulf War has severely limited Iraq's biological and chemical warfare capabilities, it has not affected Iran's programs. The US also must face the long-term prospect of Iraq recovering its capability to use weapons of mass destruction in a post-sanctions environment, and the risk that both Iran and Iraq will become nuclear powers and/or acquire biological weapons with the lethality of nuclear weapons.

As Secretary Perry's FY1996 Annual Report states:[139]

> As DoD's understanding of these major regional contingencies has developed, it became clear that there was a very high probability that aggressors would threaten, wield, or use weapons of mass destruction. Earlier assumptions that conflicts not involving the Soviet Union would be fought solely with conventional weapons needed to be reviewed and new guidance issued.... Nuclear, biological, and chemical (NBC) weapons—collectively weapons of mass destruction—are no longer a hypothetical threat in regional conflicts. Almost anywhere the US is likely to deploy forces around the world—Northeast Asia, the Gulf, the Middle East, and Europe—states are likely to have weapons of mass destruction.

The Threat of Weapons of Mass Destruction in the Gulf

Table Fourteen shows that Iran and Iraq are developing significant capabilities to develop weapons of mass destruction. At the same time, Table Fourteen shows that the present capabilities of such forces should not be exaggerated. Iran lacks a long-range delivery system capable of meaningful coverage of Israel, although it could potentially stage strike aircraft and Scuds through Syria or Jordan. At present, it does not seem to have highly effective chemical weapons or to have deployed significant numbers of biological weapons, and could not add significantly to Syrian capabilities. This situation will change, however, if Iran gets the No Dong or M-9 missile and/or develops an advanced air refueling capability, and as Iran improves the quality of its chemical and biological weapons.

The situation will also change radically if Iran acquires nuclear weapons, to which Iran seems firmly committed. It is not possible to confirm any specific Iranian sites, but Iran is clearly developing the capability to exploit its uranium resources in Yazd Province, and has experimented in uranium enrichment and centrifuge technology at its Sharif University of Technology in Tehran, and may have conducted research into Plutonium separation. It has a small 27 kilowatt Chinese-supplied neutron source research reactor, and subcritical assemblies with 900 grams of highly enriched uranium, at its Esfahan Nuclear Research Center. This center also has a heavy water zero-power reactor, a light water sub-critical reactor, and a graphite sub-critical reactor. The center may also have experimented with some aspects of nuclear weapons design. Iran has an Argentine-fueled five megawatt light water highly enriched uranium reactor operating at the University of Tehran. Iran has also demonstrated its ability to copy the sheltering and satellite deception techniques used by Iraq before the Gulf War.[140]

Iran has sought to purchase power reactors from Russia. Though denied Russian centrifuge technology as the result of US negotiations with Russia, Iran has signed an $800 million to $1 billion dollar agreement with Russia on January 8, 1995, to build at least one reactor at Bushehr—about 730 miles south of Teheran. Bushehr is the site of two incomplete reactors started by Siemens in 1976, and where work halted in 1979 with the fall of the Shah. Construction of the main buildings and steel containment vessel for one reactor had reached 85% of completion, and construction for the other was partially finished, but both reactors were damaged during the Iran-Iraq War. Russia plans to use these German facilities to build its VVER-1000 power reactors at the site, but it is unclear that it can do much more than make use of the remaining buildings. The VVER-1000 is physically very different from a Siemens 1,300 megawatt reactor, and it would probably be more costly to attempt to redesign the VVER-1000 to use German control systems and facilities than to build an entirely new reactor facility.[141]

Russia has already deployed some 150 technicians at the reactor site, and plans major shipments of material in 1995. The reactor is scheduled to be completed by the year 2000, and Russia will also train some 500 Iranian technicians. There are some uncertainties as to whether Russia will take back the plutonium-bearing spent fuel in the reactor, although recent reports indicate that it may do so.[142] Iran has shown an interest in another VVER-1000 reactor at Bushehr, in purchasing two V-213 VVER 440 power reactors and another large research reactor. Iran has already expressed an interest in buying two 300 megawatt pressurized water nuclear reactors from China similar to the Chinese plant at Zhejiang.[143]

These Iranian plans to buy reactors make little economic sense on energy grounds for a country with vast supplies of natural gas that it can use to generate electricity at 18% to 20% of the cost of nuclear electricity. They also are an extremely expensive way of substituting for domestic oil and gas demand, and compensating for the fact that Iran underprices oil to the point where the resulting increase in domestic consumption is cutting into its export capacity.

The IAEA regularly inspects declared Iranian sites, and has made two special visits to suspect sites in February, 1992 and October, 1993. The IAEA can only formally inspect declared facilities with declared nuclear material. Its visits to other facilities have not involved the kind of intrusive inspection that can do more than determine whether a major physical facility exists that seems to be dedicated to weapons use. As a result, IAEA efforts to date can neither confirm nor deny the existence of a nuclear weapons program. Further, Iran can always reject IAEA safeguards once the reactor or reactors are complete, and then use its reactors to produce plutonium.

On the other hand, Iran continues to deny it is seeking nuclear weapons, and reports that Iran had developed a $10 billion dollar plan to acquire nuclear weapons seem little more than opposition rumors.[144] At present, most experts feel that Iran has all the basic technology to build a bomb, but only has a low to moderate-level weapons design and development effort.[145] They indicate that no major weapons material and production effort have been detected. Iran seems to be at least three to five years away from acquiring a long-range missile system, and five to nine years away from acquiring a nuclear device—although it could probably develop a gun or simple implosion nuclear weapon in nine to 48 months if it could buy fissile material.

Iraq currently has only a limited potential capability to recover its past ability to produce nuclear weapons.[146] It has lost most of its capability to deliver chemical and biological weapons and there is no immediate evidence that Iraq has improved the effectiveness of its low-lethality weapon and warhead designs. Iraq is, however, devoting large resources to biological, chemical, and nuclear research efforts. It retains significant technology, and much of the chemical and biological weapons equipment it dispersed before and during Desert Storm. It also retains a long-range air strike capability and probably retains some Scud and improved Scud missile assemblies.

TABLE FOURTEEN   The Iranian and Iraqi Race for Weapons of Mass
                 Destruction in the Gulf

Iran

Delivery Systems

- Used regular Scud extensively during Iran-Iraq War. Fired nearly 100 Scud B missiles during 1985–1988. Scud missiles were provided by Libya and North Korea.
- Has 6-12 Scud launchers and up to 200 Scud B (R-17E) missiles with 230-310 KM range.
- Has new long range North Korean Scuds—with ranges near 500 kilometers.
- Has created shelters and tunnels in its coastal areas to store Scud and other missiles in hardened sites and reduce their vulnerability to air attack.
- Can now assemble missiles using foreign made components.
- Developing an indigenous missile production capability with both solid and liquid fueled missiles. Seems to be seeking capability to produce MRBMs.
- May cooperate with Syria in developing capability to manufacture missiles.
- Probably has ordered North Korean No Dong missile which can carry nuclear and biological missile ranges of up to 900 kilometers. Can reach virtually any target in Gulf, Turkey, and Israel, although CIA now estimates deliveries will only begin in 1997–1999.[147]
- Has recently bought CSS-8 surface-to-surface missiles (converted SA-2s) from China with ranges of 130–150 kilometers.
- May have placed order for PRC-made M-9 missile (280–620 kilometers range). More likely that PRC firms are giving assistance in developing indigenous missile R&D and production facilities.
- Has Chinese sea and land-based anti-ship cruise missiles. Iran fired 10 such missiles at Kuwait during Iran-Iraq War, hitting one US-flagged tanker.
- Su-24 long-range strike fighters with range-payloads roughly equivalent to US F-111 and superior to older Soviet medium bombers.
- Iranian made IRAN 130 rocket with 150+ kilometers range.
- Iranian Oghab (Eagle) rocket with 40+ kilometers range.
- New SSM with 125 mile range may be in production, but could be modified FROG.
- F-4D/E fighter bombers with capability to carry extensive payloads to ranges of 450 miles.
- Can modify HY-2 Silkworm missiles and SA-2 surface-to-air missiles to deliver weapons of mass destruction.
- Large numbers of multiple rocket launchers and tube artillery for short range delivery of chemical weapons.
- Experimenting with cruise missile development.

Chemical Weapons

- At least two major research and production facilities.

(continues)

TABLE FOURTEEN   *(continued)*

- Made limited use of chemical weapons at end of the Iran-Iraq War.
- Began to create stockpiles of cyanide (cyanogen chloride), phosgene, and mustard gas weapons after 1985. Include bombs and artillery.
- Was able to produce blister (mustard) and blood (cyanide) agents by 1987; used them in artillery shells against Iraqi troops.
- Production of nerve gas weapons started no later than 1994.
- Has produced a minimum of several hundred tons of blister, blood, and choking agents. Some are weaponized for support of ground troops. Others are used in chemical bombs.
- Has increased chemical defensive and offensive warfare training since 1993.
- Seeking to buy more advanced chemical defense equipment.
- Has sought to buy specialized equipment on world market to develop indigenous capability to produce advanced feedstocks for nerve weapons.

Biological Weapons

- Extensive laboratory and research capability.
- Weapons effort documented as early as 1982.
- Bioresearch effort sophisticated enough to produce biological weapons as lethal as small nuclear weapons. Working on toxins and organisms with biological warfare capabilities.
- Has biological support structure capable of producing many different biological weapons. Has evolved from piecemeal acquisition of biological equipment to pursuing complete biological production plants.
- Seems to have the production facilities to make dry storable weapons. This would allow it to develop suitable missile warheads and bombs and covert devices.
- May be involved in active weapons production, but no evidence to date that this is the case.
- Some universities and research centers may be linked to biological weapons program.

Nuclear Weapons

- In 1984, revived nuclear weapons program begun under Shah.
- Received significant West German and Argentine corporate support in some aspects of nuclear technology during the Iran-Iraq War.
- Limited transfers of centrifuge and other weapons related technology from PRC, possibly Pakistan.
- Stockpiles of uranium and mines in Yazd area.
- Seems to have attempted to buy fissile material from Khazakstan.
- Has sought heavy water research reactors with no application to peaceful light-water power reactor development.
- Has sought to obtain uranium enrichment and spent fuel reprocessing technology whose main applications are in weapons programs.

(continues)

TABLE FOURTEEN   *(continued)*

- Russian agreement to build up to four reactors, beginning with a complex at Bushehr—with two 1,000–1,200 megawatt reactors and two 465 megawatt reactors, and provide significant nuclear technology.
- Chinese agreement to provide significant nuclear technology transfer and possible sale of two 300 megawatt pressurized water reactors.
- No way to tell when current efforts will produce a weapon, and unclassified lists of potential facilities have little credibility. We simply do not know where Iran is developing its weapons.
- IAEA has found no indications of weapons effort, but found no efforts in Iraq in spring of 1990. IAEA only formally inspects Iran's small research reactors. Its visits to other Iranian sites are not thorough enough to confirm or deny whether Iran has such activities.
- Timing of weapons acquisition depends heavily on whether Iran can buy fissile material—if so it has the design capability and can produce weapons in 1–2 years—or must develop the capability to process Plutonium or enrich Uranium—in which case, it is likely to be 5–10 years.

Iraq

Delivery Systems

- Delivery systems at the time of the Gulf War included:
  - Tu-16 and Tu-22 bombers.
  - MiG-29 fighters.
  - Mirage F-1, MiG-23BM, and Su-22 fighter attack aircraft.
  - A Scud force with a minimum of 819 missiles.
  - Extended range Al-Hussein Scud variants (600 kilometer range) extensively deployed throughout Iraq, and at three fixed sites in northern, western, and southern Iraq.
  - Developing Al-Abbas missiles (900 kilometer range) Al-Abbas which could reach targets in Iran, the Persian Gulf, Israel, Turkey, and Cyprus.
  - Long-range super guns with ranges of up to 600 kilometers.
- Iraq had long-range strike aircraft with refueling capabilities and several hundred regular and improved, longer-range Scud missiles, some with chemical warheads.
- Iraq fired 84 Al-Husayns, 3 Al Husyan-Shorts, and 1 Al-Hijrarah (with a cement warhead) during the Gulf War.
- The Gulf War deprived Iraq of some of its MiG-29s, Mirage F-1s, MiG-23BMs, and Su-22s. Since the end of the war, the UN inspection regime has also destroyed many of Iraq's long-range missiles.
- Iraq, however, maintains a significant delivery capability consisting of:
  - HY-2, SS-N-2, and C-601 cruise missiles, which are unaffected by UN cease-fire terms.

(continues)

TABLE FOURTEEN   (*continued*)

- FROG-7 rockets with 70 kilometer ranges, also allowed under UN resolutions.
- Multiple rocket launchers and tube artillery.
- Several Scud launchers
- US experts believe Iran may still have components for several dozen extended-range Scud missiles. UN experts believe Iraq is concealing up to Scud 6–7 launchers and 11–24 missile assemblies.
- Iraq has focused its missile programs around the Scud B. During the late 1980s, it began to enlarge the fuel tanks of its Scuds and reduce the weight of its warheads to extend their range beyond the normal 300 kilometer maximum range of the Scud. It also developed a capability to manufacture Scud variants in Iraq, and was working on production facilities for a development of the solid-fueled Argentine Condor missile called the Badr 2000.
- Iraqi missile programs at the time of the Gulf War included:
  - Scud Bs with a maximum range of 300 kilometers.
  - Al Husayns with a 600–650 range.
  - Al Husayn-Shorts (a variant of the Al Husayn) with a 600–650 range
  - Al Hijarahs with a 600–650 range
- Iraqi developmental missile programs at the time of the Gulf War included:
  - Al Fahd. A conversion of the SA-2 with an intended 300 kilometer range. Abandoned in the R&D phase.
  - Extended-range Al Fahd. A 500 kilometer range missile abandoned in the development phase after exhibition at the 1989 arms show in Baghdad.
  - Al Abbas. A longer version of the Al Husayn with a lighter warhead which was intended to have a 900 kilometer range. Abandoned during R&D.
  - Badr 2000. A solid-propellant two-stage missile based on the Condor with a range of 750–1,000 kilometers. Was in R&D when Gulf War began. Facilities were constructed to begin missile production.
  - Tammouz 1: a missile based on the Scud with an SA-2 sustainer for a second stage. It had an intended range of 2,000 kilometers but was not carried through to advanced R&D.
  - Al Abid: A three stage space vehicle with a first stage of 5 Al Abbas airframes. Test launch in December 1989.
- Iraq also engaged in effort to develop a solid fueled missile with a similar range to the Tammouz.
- Clear evidence that at least one Iraqi long-range missile design was to have a nuclear warhead.
- Iraq attempted to conceal a plant making missile engines from the UN inspectors. It only admitted this plant existed in 1995, raising new questions about how many of its missiles have been destroyed.
- Iraq produced or assembled 80 Scud missiles it its own factories. Some 53 seem to have been unusable, but 10 are still unaccounted for.
- Had design work underway for a nuclear warhead for its long range missiles.

(*continues*)

TABLE FOURTEEN   *(continued)*

- In addition, Iraq has admitted to:
  - Hiding its capability to manufacture its own Scuds.
  - Iraq claims to have manufactured only 80 missile assemblies, 53 of which were unusable. UNSCOM claims that 10 are unaccounted for.
  - Developing an extended range variant of the FROG-7 called the Laith. The UN claims to have tagged all existing FROG-7s to prevent any extension of their range beyond the UN imposed limit of 150 kilometers for Iraqi missiles.
  - Experimenting with cruise missile technology and ballistic missile designs with ranges up to 3,000 kilometers.
  - Flight testing Al-Hussein missiles with chemical warheads in April 1990.
  - Initiating a research and development program for a nuclear warhead missile delivery system.
  - Successfully developing and testing a warhead separation system.
  - Indigenously developing, testing, and manufacturing advanced rocket engines to include liquid-propellant designs.
  - Conducting research into the development of Remotely Piloted Vehicles (RPVs) for the dissemination of biological agents.
  - Attempting to expand its Ababil-100 program designed to build surface-to-surface missiles with ranges beyond the permitted 100–150 kilometers.
  - Starting an indigenous 600 mm supergun design effort.
- US and UN officials conclude further that:
  - Iraq is concentrating procurement efforts on rebuilding its ballistic missile program using a clandestine network of front companies to obtain the necessary materials and technology from European and Russian firms.
  - This equipment is then concealed and stockpiled for assembly concomitant with the end of the UN inspection regime.
  - The equipment clandestinely sought by Iraq includes advanced missile guidance components, such as accelerometers and gyroscopes, specialty metals, special machine tools, and a high-tech, French-made, million-dollar furnace designed to fabricate engine parts for missiles.
- Jordan found that Iraq was smuggling missile components through Jordan in early December 1995.
- US satellite photographs reveal that Iraq has rebuilt its Al-Kindi missile research facility.
- Iraq retains the technology it acquired before the war and evidence clearly indicates an ongoing research and development effort, in spite of the UN sanctions regime.
- The fact that UN Security Council Resolution 687 allows Iraq to continue producing and testing short range missiles (less than 150 kilometers range) has meant it can retain significant missile efforts. Iraq's on-going rocket and missile programs include:
  - Luna/Frog-7. A Russian unguided rocket with a 70 kilometer range currently in service and in limited production.

(continues)

TABLE FOURTEEN   *(continued)*

- Astros II. A Brazilian unguided rocket with a 60 kilometer range currently in service and in limited production.
- SA-2. A Russian surface-to-air missile which China has demonstrated can be converted into a 300 kilometer range surface-to-surface missile.
- SA-3. A Russian surface-to-air missile which has some potential for conversion to a surface-to-surface missile.
- Ababil-50. An Yugoslav-designed Iraqi-produced 50 kilometer range artillery rocket with very limited growth potential.
- Ababil-100. An Iraqi 100–150 kilometer range system with parallel solid-fuel and liquid fuel development programs which seems to be used as a "legal" test-bed and foundation for much longer range missile programs once sanctions are lifted. Many of the liquid fueled programs are compatible with Scud production.
- Limited stocks of French and Chinese produced land and air launched cruise missiles.

Chemical Weapons

- Produced several thousand tons of chemical weapons from 1984 on. Used chemical weapons extensively against Iran and its own Kurdish population in 1988.
- Use of Tabun gas against Iranians beginning in 1984 is first confirmed use of nerve agents in war.
- Had roughly 1,000 metric tons of chemical weapons on hand at time invaded Kuwait, split equally between blister agents and nerve agents.
- UN destruction efforts at Samara destroyed over 27,000 chemical bombs, rockets, and artillery shells, including 30 Scud missile warheads. About 500 tons of mustard and nerve agents, and thousands of tons of precursor chemicals were burned or chemically neutralized.
- In revelations to the UN, Iraq admitted that, prior to the Gulf War, it:
  - Maintained large stockpiles of mustard gas, and the nerve agents Sarin and Tabun.
  - Produced binary Sarin filled artillery shells, 122 mm rockets, and aerial bombs.
  - Manufactured enough precursors to produce 490 tons of the nerve agent VX. These precursors included 65 tons of choline and 200 tons of phosphorous pentasulfide and di-isopropylamine
  - Tested Ricin, a deadly nerve agent, for use in artillery shells.
  - Had three flight tests of long range Scuds with chemical warheads.
  - Had large VX production effort underway at the time of the Gulf War. The destruction of the related weapons and feedstocks has been claimed by Iraq, but not verified by UNSCOM.
- The majority of Iraq's chemical agents were manufactured at a supposed pesticide plant located at Samara. Various, other production facilities were also

(continues)

TABLE FOURTEEN   (*continued*)

used, including those at Salman Pak, Muthanna, and Habbiniyah. Though severely damaged during the war, the physical plant for many of these facilities has been rebuilt.
  • Iraq possessed the technology to produce a variety of other persistent and non-persistent agents.
• The Gulf War and subsequent
  • UN inspection regime may have largely eliminated these stockpiles and reduced production capability.
  • US experts believe Iraq has concealed significant stocks of precursors. It also appears to retain significant amounts of production equipment dispersed before, or during, Desert Storm and not recovered by the UN.
• Iraq has developed basic chemical warhead designs for Scud missiles, rockets, bombs, and shells. Iraq also has spray dispersal systems.
• Iraq maintains extensive stocks of defensive equipment.
• The UN maintains that Iraq is not currently producing chemical agents, but the UN is also concerned that Iraq has offered no evidence that it has destroyed its VX production capability and/or stockpile.
• Further, Iraq retains the technology it acquired before the war and evidence clearly indicates an ongoing research and development effort, in spite of the UN sanctions regime.

Biological Weapons

• Systematically lied about biological weapons effort until 1995. First stated that had small defensive efforts, but no offensive effort. In July 1995, admitted had a major offensive effort. In October 1995, finally admitted major weaponization effort.
• The August 1995 defection of Lieutenant General Hussein Kamel Majid, formerly in charge of Iraq's weapons of mass destruction, led Iraq to reveal the extent of its biological weapons program.
• Iraq reported to the UN in August 1995 that it had produced 90,000 liters of Botulinium toxin, 8,300 liters of Anthrax, and significant quantities of other agents.
• Iraq has, however, continued to lie about its biological weapons effort.
• It has claimed the effort is headed by Dr. Taha, a woman who only headed a subordinate effort. It has not admitted to any help by foreign personnel or contractors. It has claimed to have destroyed its weapons, but the one site UNSCOM inspectors visited showed no signs of such destruction and was later said to be the wrong site. It has claimed only 50 people were employed full time, but the scale of the effort would have required several hundred.
• Reports indicate that Iraq tested at least 7 principal biological agents for use against humans.
  • Anthrax, Botulinum, and Aflatoxin known to be weaponized.
  • Looked at viruses, bacteria, and fungi. Examined the possibility of weaponizing Gas Gangrene and Mycotoxins. Some field trials were held of these agents.

(*continues*)

TABLE FOURTEEN   *(continued)*

- Examined foot and mouth disease, haemorrhagic conjunctivitis virus, rotavirus, and camel pox virus.
- Conducted research on a "wheat pathogen" and a Mycotoxin similar to "yellow rain" defoliant.
- The "wheat smut" was first produced at Al Salman, and then put in major production during 1987–1988 at a plant near Mosul. Iraq claims the program was abandoned.
- The defection of Hussein Kamel prompted Iraq to admit that it:
  - Imported 39 tons of growth media for biological agents obtained from three European firms. According to UNSCOM, 17 tons remains unaccounted for. Each ton can be used to produce 10 tons of bacteriological weapons.
  - Imported type cultures which can be modified to develop biological weapons from the US.
  - Had a laboratory- and industrial-scale capability to manufacture various biological agents including the bacteria which cause anthrax and botulism; Aflatoxin, a naturally occurring carcinogen; clostridium perfringens, a gangrene-causing agent; the protein toxin ricin; tricothecene mycotoxins, such as T-2 and DAS; and an anti-wheat fungus known as wheat cover smut. Iraq also conducted research into the rotavirus, the camel pox virus and the virus which causes haemorrhagic conjunctivitis.
  - Created at least seven primary production facilities including the Sepp Institute at Muthanna, the Ghazi Research Institute at Amaria, the Daura Foot and Mouth Disease Institute, and facilities at Al-Hakim, Salman Pak Taji, and Fudaliyah. According to UNSCOM, weaponization occurred primarily at Muthanna through May 1987 (largely Botulinum), and then moved to Al Salman. (Anthrax). In March 1988 a plant was open at Al Hakim, and in 1989 an Aflatoxin plant was set up at Fudaliyah.
  - Manufactured 6,000 liters of concentrated Botulinum toxin and 8,425 liters of anthrax at Al-Hakim during 1990; 5400 liters of concentrated Botulinum toxin at the Daura Foot and Mouth Disease Institute from November 1990 to January 15, 1991; 400 liters of concentrated Botulinum toxin at Taji; and 150 liters of concentrated anthrax at Salman Pak. Produced 1,850 liters of Aflatoxin in solution at Fudaliyah.
  - Produced 340 liters of concentrated clostridium perfringens, a gangrene-causing biological agent, beginning in August 1990.
  - Produced 10 liters of concentrated Ricin at Al Salam. Claim abandoned work after tests failed.
  - Relocated much of its biological weapons effort after Coalition strikes on its facilities at Al Kindi and Salman Pak to Al Hakim and other facilities. This makes tracking the weapons effort extremely difficult.
  - Had at least 79 civilian facilities capable of playing some role in biological weapons production still extent in 1995.
- Extensive weaponization program

(continues)

TABLE FOURTEEN   (*continued*)

- Conducted field trials, weaponization tests, and live firings of 122 mm rockets armed with anthrax and Botulinum toxin from March 1988 to May 1990.
- Total production reached at least 19,000 liters of concentrated Botulinum (10,000 liters filled into munitions); 8,500 liters of concentrated Anthrax (6,500 liters filled into munitions); and 2,500 liters of concentrated Aflatoxin (1,850 liters filled into munitions).
- Weaponized at least three biological agents for use in the Gulf War. The weaponization consisted of 100 bombs and 15 missile warheads loaded with Botulinum; 50 R-400 air-delivered bombs and 10 missile warheads loaded with anthrax.
- Also had 16 missile warheads loaded with Aflatoxin, a natural carcinogen. The warheads were designed for operability with the Al-Hussein Scud variant.
- A total of at least 166 bombs were filled with some biological agent. Iraq produced at least 191 bombs and missile warheads with biological agents.
- Developed and stored drops tanks ready for use for three aircraft or RPV s with the capability of dispersing 2,000 liters of anthrax. Development took place in December 1990. Claimed later that tests showed were ineffective.
- Tested ricin, a deadly protein toxin, for use in artillery shells.
- The UN claims that Iraq has offered no evidence to corroborate its claims that it destroyed its stockpile of biological agents after the Gulf War. Further, Iraq retains the technology it acquired before the war and evidence clearly indicates an ongoing research and development effort, in spite of the UN sanctions regime.
- UN currently inspects 79 sites—5 used to make weapons before war; 5 vaccine or pharmaceutical sites; 35 research and university sites; thirteen breweries, distilleries, and dairies with dual-purpose capabilities; eight diagnostic laboratories.
- Retains laboratory capability to manufacture various biological agents including the bacteria which cause anthrax, botulism, tularemia and typhoid.
- Many additional civilian facilities capable of playing some role in biological weapons production.

Nuclear Weapons

- Sought to buy a plutonium production reactor similar to the reactor France used in its nuclear weapons program in early 1970s.
- Contracted with France to build Osirak and Isis reactors in 1976, as part of Tuwaitha complex near Baghdad.
- Osirak raid in June 1981 prevented from acquiring reactors for weapons use. Led Iraq to refocus efforts on producing highly enriched uranium.
- Inspections by UN teams have found evidence of two successful weapons designs, a neutron initiator, explosives and triggering technology needed for production of bombs, plutonium processing technology, centrifuge technology, Calutron enrichment technology, and experiments with chemical separation technology.

(*continues*)

TABLE FOURTEEN   *(continued)*

- Iraq used Calutron, centrifuges, plutonium processing, chemical defusion and foreign purchases to create new production capability after Israel destroyed most of Osiraq.
- Iraq established a centrifuge enrichment system in Rashidya and conducted research into the nuclear fuel cycle to facilitate development of a nuclear device.
- After invading Kuwait, Iraq attempted to accelerate its program to develop a nuclear weapon by using radioactive fuel from French and Russian-built reactors.
- Made a crash effort beginning in September 1990 to recover enriched fuel from its supposedly safe-guarded French and Russian reactors, with the goal of produced a nuclear weapon by April 1991. The program was only halted after Coalition air raid destroyed key facilities on January 17, 1991.
- Iraq conducted research into the production of a radiological weapon, which disperses lethal radioactive material without initiating a nuclear explosion.
  - Orders were given in 1987 to explore the use of radiological weapons for area denial in the Iran-Iraq War.
  - Three prototype bombs were detonated at test sites—one as a ground level static test and two others were dropped from aircraft.
  - Iraq claims the results were disappointing and the project was shelved but has no records or evidence to prove this.
- UN teams have found and destroyed, or secured, new stockpiles of illegal enriched material, major production and R&D facilities, and equipment—including Calutron enriching equipment.
- UNSCOM believes that Iraq's nuclear program has been largely disabled and remains incapacitated, but warns that Iraq retains substantial technology and established a clandestine purchasing system in 1990 that it has used to import forbidden components since the Gulf War.
- Iraq still retains the technology developed before the Gulf War and US experts believe an ongoing research and development effort continues, in spite of the UN sanctions regime.
- A substantial number of declared nuclear weapons components and research equipment has never been recovered. There is no reason to assume that Iraqi declarations were comprehensive.

Source: Prepared by Anthony H. Cordesman, Co-Director, Middle East Program, CSIS.

In short, the immediate threat posed by the capabilities of nations like Iran, and Iran does not radically alter the regional military balance, but the steady process of proliferation does. The US and its Gulf allies can scarcely plan on the basis that such nations will radically change their behavior in the near-term, or ignore the mid-term risks that they pose in arms control planning.

Table Fifteen illustrates just how lethal future Iranian and Iraqi capabilities can be. The chemical weapons in this table may not have anything approaching the destructive power of biological and nuclear weapons. However, they cannot be disregarded—particularly if an attacking state should use aircraft or cruise missiles to deliver such weapons in aerosol form—rather than in the far less lethal form likely to result from ballistic missile attacks. Chemical weapons could still radically alter the nature of the escalation and targeting in a future Arab-Israeli conflict. At the same time, they cannot threaten the survival of states in their current form.

In contrast, biological weapons are a true weapon of mass destruction. They can be as destructive as small nuclear weapons, and both Iran and Iraq have biological weapons efforts. Further, covert delivery of such weapons is by far the most lethal way of using them. It would take a very advanced ballistic missile warhead to disseminate a survivable and fully lethal biological agent over a wide area at the right height. At the same time, crude unconventional delivery systems like releasing a biological agent from a ship, roof top, or commercial aircraft can be very effective.

The US, for example, experimented during the Cold War by dispersing inert particulate matter the same size and weight as Anthrax spores. It delivered such spores from commercial vessels moving along the coast of New Jersey and in "terrorist" attacks sprinkling the spores over commuters rushing home through Grand Central Station in New York. Both dissemination systems were very effective and would have produced very high death rates. Both would have required human intelligence identifying the attackers in advance to prevent heavy losses. Metal detectors and other technological means would not have been effective, and most conventional anti-terrorist protective measures would have failed.

The effects of biological and nuclear weapons should not be exaggerated, but many of the Southern Gulf states are literally "one bomb" states. A single nuclear device could destroy a majority of the population, particularly under conditions where increases in the long-term death rate were included in the estimate of casualties shown in Table Fourteen—which currently only includes short-term deaths within a 48 hour to seven day period. At the same time, a nuclear attack on the capital of any of the states just listed could destroy its current political leadership, much of its economy, and a great deal of the state's cohesion and national identity. Recovery would be questionable, and the social and economic impact of any such strike would last a decade or more.

Advances in technology also present growing problems. There have been no breakthroughs in the production of fissile material, but there is a vast amount of fissile material in the former Soviet Union, and more and more countries could produce an aircraft deliverable nuclear device in a matter of a few months or years if they could buy weapons-grade material.

TABLE FIFTEEN   The Comparative Effects of Biological, Chemical, and Nuclear Weapons Delivered Against a Typical Urban Target in the Middle East

Using missile warheads: Assumes one Scud sized warhead with a maximum payload of 1,000 kilograms. The study assumes that the biological agent would not make maximum use of this payload capacity because the country deploying such systems cannot make an efficient warhead. It is unclear if this assumption is realistic.

	Area Covered in Square Kilometers	Deaths Assuming 3,000–10,000 People Per Square Kilometer
Chemical: 300 kilograms of Sarin nerve gas with a density of 70 milligrams per cubic meter	0.22	60–200
Biological: 30 kilograms of Anthrax spores with a density of 0.1 milligram per cubic meter	10	30,000–100,000
Nuclear:		
One 12.5 kilotron nuclear device achieving 5 pounds per cubic inch of over-pressure	7.8	23,000–80,000
One 1 megaton hydrogen bomb	190	570,000–1,900,000

Using one aircraft delivering 1,000 kilograms of Sarin nerve gas or 100 kilograms of anthrax spores: Assumes the aircraft flies in a straight line over the target at optimal altitude, and dispenses the agent as an aerosol. The study assumes that the biological agent would not make maximum use of the weapons weight carrying capacity. It is unclear this assumption is realistic.

	Area Covered in Square Kilometers	Deaths Assuming 3,000–10,000 People Per Square Kilometer
Clear sunny day, light breeze		
Sarin Nerve Gas	0.74	300–700
Anthrax Spores	46.00	130,000–460,000
Overcast day or night, moderate wind		
Sarin Nerve Gas	0.8	400–800
Anthrax Spores	140.00	420,000–1,400,000
Clear calm night		
Sarin Nerve Gas	7.8	3,000–8,000
Anthrax Spores	300.00	1,000,000–3,000,000

Source: Adapted by the author from Office of Technology Assessment, *Proliferation of Weapons of Mass Destruction: Assessing the Risks,* US Congress OTA-ISC-559, Washington, August 1993, pp. 53–54.

The very nature of biotechnology means all of the countries in the Middle East are steadily acquiring the capability to make extremely lethal, dry-storable biological weapons, and to do so with fewer and fewer indicators in terms of imports of specialized technology, with more use of dual-use or civilian production facilities, and in smaller spaces.

Long-range ballistic missile systems are being deployed in Iran and Iraq, and more will follow the moment UN sanctions end. Better strike fighters—often with performance capabilities superior to yesterday's bombers—are already being deployed. The kind of cruise missile technology suited to long-range delivery of both nuclear and biological weapons against area targets like cities is becoming available.

All of these developments have dangerous war-fighting effects. Nations like Iran and Iraq that are in the process of acquiring a few nuclear weapons or serious biological weapons tend to see wars involving such weapons in terms of threats to enemy population centers and often feel they have little option other than to strike or concede if intimidation fails. They also keep their capabilities covert, and scarcely debate the potential use of such weapons as part of their normal process of decision making. This approach to acquiring truly lethal weapons of mass destruction can lead to rapid massive escalation or surprise attacks—particularly if Iran or Iraq fears preemption, structures its forces to launch under attack, and/or seeks to strike before its opponent can bring its retaliatory forces and air and missile defenses to full readiness. Fewer weapons do not mean great stability and security, and they almost inevitably mean counter-value targeting.

As the East-West arms race showed, there also is no logical stopping point in such an arms race. Broadening the number and type of weapons to allow strikes against military targets creates an incentive to be able to strike as many targets as possible. Obtaining the option to strike at tactical military targets lowers the threshold of escalation and may lead a given side to be more willing to attack. Reducing the vulnerability of steadily larger inventories of weapons and delivery systems may lead to a loss of control, or more lethal plans to preempt or launch under attack. Larger forces potentially increase the risk that weapons directed against military targets will hit population centers. Further, a state under existential attack by one neighbor may lash out against other states—a pattern Iraq already has exhibited by launching missile attacks against Israel during the Gulf War.

The existence of such "worst-case" risks does not make them probable. Rational, moderate leaders do not take existential risks or escalate to genocidal conflicts. At the same time, it is difficult to say that proliferation leads to predictable crisis behavior or escalation ladders. Further, they create problems in terms of establishing any clear limits as to how the potential use of given types of weapons of mass destruction—like chemical weapons—relate to the use of biological weapons and nuclear weapons. There are no clear rules, particularly when few leaders in the region will understand the effects of such weapons and the possible consequences of using them, and have anything like the damage assessment and command and control systems necessary to manage escalation once it begins. These uncertainties mean that the US must at least consider worst-case contingencies.

US Responses to the Problem of Counterproliferation

In the near-term, the US can deal with the threats posed by Iran and Iraq by a combination of missile and air defense, using the Patriot and other US and regional air defenses, retaliatory threats or strikes, using conventional air and missile power, and passive defense measures like chemical protection gear. It is doubtful, however, that such measures will be adequate much beyond the early 2000s, and it is increasingly doubtful that arms control measures and efforts to limit technology transfer to Iran and Iraq offer the US and the Southern Gulf states even mid-term security against Iran and Iraq.

Such defenses are already inadequate in dealing with biological warfare. In a recent war game and simulation at the US Naval War College, planners found that the US would be unable to prevent massive military and civilian casualties in the event of a determined attack by a power like Iran and Iraq. One of the main concerns raised by the exercise was that the US pharmaceutical industry lacked a sufficient stockpile of vaccines and antidotes to inoculate against biological toxins. The exercise found that forced rationing of these antidotes would create serious logistical, operational, and moral problems for US commanders. Other exercises have shown that similar problems may emerge in defense against nuclear and advanced chemical attacks.[148]

The US has begun to develop a more effective counterproliferation doctrine as part of the Bottom Up Review, but this effort has been slow, has often had a somewhat theoretical character, and has sometimes substituted rhetoric for reality. As part of US effort during the last two years, however, the US has formed a new Counterproliferation Support Program. This Program is intended to bring a new degree of coordination to some $3 billion worth of on-going programs that affect some aspect of counterproliferation, including theater ballistic missile defense. The Department has also requested $108 million in new funding for the office in FY1996.[149] Moreover, it has begun to develop a more precise set of goals for counterproliferation that can be applied to specific military capabilities in the Gulf.

Secretary Perry listed eight possible US responses in dealing with the problem of proliferation in his FY1996 annual report:[150]

- Dissuasion to convince non-weapons of mass destruction states that their security interests are best served through not acquiring weapons of mass destruction.
- Denial to curtail access to technology and materials for weapons of mass destruction through export controls and other tools,
- Arms control efforts to reinforce the Nuclear Non-Proliferation Treaty, Biological and Chemical Weapons Conventions, nuclear free zones, conventional arms treaties that stabilize arms races, confidence and security building measures, and Anti-Ballistic Missile Treaty clarification efforts to allow US deployment of advanced theater ballistic missile defenses.
- International pressure to punish violators with trade sanctions, to publicize and expose companies and countries that assist proliferators, and to share intelligence to heighten awareness of the proliferation problem.
- Defusing potentially dangerous situations by undertaking actions to reduce the threat from weapons of mass destruction already in the hands of selected countries—such as agreements to destroy, inspect, convert, monitor, or even reverse their capabilities.
- Military capabilities to be prepared to seize, disable, or destroy weapons of mass destruction in time of conflict.
- Defensive capabilities, both active (theater missile defenses) and passive (protective gear and vaccines) that will mitigate or neutralize the effects of weapons of mass destruction and enable US forces to fight effectively even on a contaminated battlefield.

Iran and Iraq are highly unlikely to be deterred from pursuing weapons of massive destruction through political persuasion and arms control—although such efforts continue to have high priority. This leaves the US and its allies with the options of seeking to prevent technology and weapons transfer, creating military capabilities to seize or destroy Iranian and Iraqi weapons of mass destruction in a conflict, and creating defensive capabilities in the region.

Force Improvements Affecting Counterproliferation Capability

The US has not announced a comprehensive program for acting on these options. In fact, the US has had considerable difficulty in defining the exact programs that it should fund. The Department of Defense has made it clear, however, that it does seek to improve related intelligence, battlefield surveillance, passive defense, active defense, and counter-force capabilities, as well as related counter-terrorism, export control and arms control inspection activities. US work on counterproliferation has identified 16 priority technologies and 14 war fighting capabilities where the US must make improvements in its counterproliferation capabilities.

These war fighting capabilities have been selected as part of the Joint Staff's Warfighting Capabilities Assessment (JWCA) process and include detection and tracking shipments, intercepting cruise missiles, prompt kill of mobile targets, planning and targeting above ground infrastructure, characterizing and identifying underground targets, defeating underground targets, support for special operations, improved intelligence support, better passive defense operations, improved NBC operations capability, chemical and biological weapons detection and characterization, production of biological warfare vaccines, defeating biological and chemical agents, and detecting, locating, and disarming weapons of mass destruction overseas and in the US. The US also made counterproliferation a military mission as part of its Unified Command Plan on May 24, 1995.[151]

These technologies and war fighting capabilities can be grouped into seven areas where US capabilities need major improvement:[152]

- *Detection and characterization of biological and chemical agents.* This initiative is intended to accelerate the fielding of stand-off and point-detection and characterization systems by up to six years. It also addresses the integration of sensors into existing and planned carrier platforms, emphasizing man-portability and compatibility with UAVs.

- *Detection, characterization, and defeat of hard, underground targets.* The US is seeking new sensors, enhanced lethality, and penetrating weapons to increase the probability of defeating the target while minimizing the risk of collateral damage.

- *Detection, localization and neutralization of weapons of mass destruction inside and outside the US.* The US is seeking to identify and evaluate systems, force structures, and operational plans to protect key military facilities and logistic nodes, and conduct joint exercises to improve the capability to respond to potential biological and chemical threats.

- *Development and deployment of additional passive defense capabilities for US forces, including development and production of biological agent vaccines.* This program will develop and field improved protective suits, shelters, filter systems, and equipment two to five years faster than previously planned. It also restores funding to the development of improved decontamination methods.

- *Support for weapons of mass destruction-related armed control measures include strengthening the NNPT, CTB, and BWC.* They include establishing a COCOM successor regime, and improving controls on exports and technology by strengthening the MTCR, Nuclear Suppliers Group and Australia Group.
- *Missile defense capabilities, with primary emphasis on theater ballistic missile defenses.* This activity involves improvements in active and passive defenses, attack operations, and improvements in BM/C^{4}I as well as the deployment of theater missile defenses. The primary focus, however, is on anti-ballistic missile defenses, and in the near-term, this involves the development of the Patriot Advanced Capability Level-3 (PAC-3/ERINT), Navy area theater missile defense (Aegis), and theater high altitude area defense (THAAD).

The US spent about $60 million on its counterproliferation support program in FY1995. It planned to spend about $108 million in FY1996—with $5 million on systems analysis and architecture studies, $9.3 million on battlefield surveillance, $4.9 million on countering covert threats to use weapons of mass destruction, $2.8 million on proliferation prevention, $52.5 million on counterforce capabilities, and $33.7 million on passive defense.[153]

The US gave new early deployment priority to programs to detect and characterize biological and chemical weapons beginning in FY1995—including programs using new UAVs and protected vehicles. As part of its FY1996 and FY1997 programs, it began to deploy new emitter identifiers to identify and track ships carrying NBC-related cargoes. It accelerated the long-range biological stand-off detector system, and joint lightweight protective suit program. It improved its targeting systems to attack NBC facilities and minimize collateral damage. It improved intelligence support for counterproliferation efforts, strengthened cooperative programs with allied forces, and continued to invest heavily in new theater missile defense programs.

The US, however, deferred most other major new program initiatives until FY1998–FY1999, partly because of the need to allocate resources to conventional programs and partly because of the need to eliminate duplicative and low-priority research efforts and to focus on specific options to correct the gaps in existing US capabilities.[154]

Two major Department of Defense study groups are due to report on progress in these areas in 1996, and their recommendations will have major implications for USCENTCOM and allied capabilities in the Gulf. It seems likely that the US military services will focus on a number of new programs to further improve their capability to use strike aircraft against weapons of mass destruction. These programs will reinforce ongoing efforts that include the development and deployment of improved sensors, ELINT capabilities, and intelligence collection assets, along with the ability to conduct 24 hour operations and respond to new targeting data at a near real-time pace.

US military planners already emphasize the need for the early arrival of an integrated missile defense, and the Congress has placed a new emphasis on theater missile defense (TMD) in its mark-up of the FY1996 defense budget. Such a system is seen as performing three critical roles: reinforcing the deterrence of the use of weapons of mass destruction, providing active counterproliferation defenses in combat, and protecting the infrastructure, ports, prepositioned equipment, and allied forces necessary to support forces deploying from CONUS and outside the theater.[155] One result of this US effort is likely to be the recommendation that that the Southern Gulf states develop an integrated theater ballistic missile defense system to supplement or replace their present IHawk and Patriot surface-to-air missiles.

The US Army, Navy, and Air Force all have programs to provide theater missile defenses. These include the US Navy upper and lower-tier missile defense programs like the Lightweight Exoatmospheric Projectile (LEAP), the US Army Theater High Altitude Area Defense (THAAD), US Army Patriot Advanced Capability-3 (PAC-3) upgrade, and USAF airborne laser program. The US currently plans to spend about $10.2 billion between 1996 and 2001 on core programs like the US Navy upper-tier missile defense program with the lightweight exoatmospheric projectile, the US Army THAAD, and the US Army Patriot Advanced Capability-3 upgrade. The new Patriot system is expected to be ready by 1998, the Navy's lightweight exoatmospheric projectile by 1999, and THADD by 2002.[156]

- The LEAP missile would be carried aboard Ageis ships, be launched by the Standard SM-2 Block IVA missile-air defense missile, and have a defensive radius of 600–1,000 kilometers. It would be a long range interceptor designed to kill ballistic missile warheads at exoatmospheric ranges and long before they reached their targets. It could be fielded in the late 1990s.
- The Navy's area defense missile would also be carried aboard AEGIS ships and have a defensive radius of 100–200 kilometers. It would use the Standard SM-2 Block IVA missile-air defense missile without the added LEAP stage and would provide air and cruise missile defense, as well as ballistic missile defense. It could be fielded in the late 1990s.
- The THAAD would be an air deployable system with a defensive radius of about 300 kilometers. It would be a hit to kill system

designed to kill ballistic missile warheads at exoatmospheric ranges and long before they reached their targets. It could be fielded between 2004 and 2006.

- The PAC-3 would also be an air-deployable land-based system with a defensive radius of about 35 kilometers. It would use the new Extended Range Interceptor (ERINT) missile. It would provide air and cruise missile defense, as well as ballistic missile defense. It could be fielded as early as 1999.
- The US Army is also participating in an international cooperative program called MEADS to provide short-range protection for mobile ground troops.

These theater missile defense programs all offer significant potential benefits, but they raise serious questions about their area defense capability, because the US is currently placing on the wide-area defense coverage of THADD and Aegis to eliminate any risk it may violate the ABM Treaty. This may be the equivalent of "overkill" in terms of arms limitations and "underkill" in terms of effective missile defense. It could sharply degrade the effectiveness of US missile defense efforts, and may make area-defense of a region like the Gulf unaffordable.

Further, the Army and Navy are engaging in a growing debate over the relative ability of LEAP and THADD to provide coverage in areas like the Gulf. Some Department of Defense reports have argued that LEAP could provide coverage before THADD and the PAC-3 could be deployed. The Army has challenged whether the LEAP missile can actually destroy enemy warheads and whether the SPY-1 radar using by the Aegis ships launching the LEAP missile can actually discriminate the targets at the ranges required.[157] These debates over arms control and the priority to be given to specific programs could have a major impact in degrading or delaying the availability of theater missile defenses in the Gulf.

The Issue of Extended Deterrence

It is also important to note that one important option for counterproliferation is missing from the previous list. The US can also attempt to deal with the problem of Iranian and Iraqi proliferation through the threat of conventional or nuclear retaliation. The US demonstrated its potential capabilities for conventional retaliation during its strategic strikes against Iraq during the Gulf War, but it has never publicly stated that it has a doctrine of conventional strategic retaliation to deal with Iranian or Iraqi use of weapons of mass destruction.

Similarly, the US has been ambiguous in dealing with nuclear guarantees. The US Nuclear Posture Review of 1993 concluded that,[158] the US does not have a purely national deterrent posture, it extended the deterrent posture of its nuclear arsenal to its allies. A very progressive aspect of US nuclear posture is that it is, in part, an international posture. The NPR strongly supports continued commitment to NATO and Pacific allies.

The omission of any mention of extending the US nuclear umbrella to cover the Gulf and Middle East does not mean that the US would not do so. In 1990, President Bush and Secretary Baker at least implied that the US might use such weapons in response to an Iraqi use of weapons of mass destruction during the Gulf War. On April 26, 1996, Secretary Perry hinted that the US might use nuclear weapons to deal with the chemical threat from Libya, although his press spokesman later stressed conventional options.[159] Further, the Joint Staff directed in their Joint Strategic Capabilities Plan beginning in 1992 that US forces should target weapons of mass destruction in "threat" states and USCENTCOM is known to have assisted the US Strategic Command in identifying suitable threat states and targets. This has led to reports that targets in states like Iran and Iraq are included in the Single Integrated Operational Plan (SIOP) used for nuclear targeting.[160]

US officials may well feel that any public statement that the US might use nuclear weapons in regional contingencies would do more to provoke hostile states into proliferating than to deter their use of weapons of mass destruction, and that any such US threats should be carefully targeted to deal with specific contingencies. Nevertheless, it is far from clear that the US now has a well-defined doctrine for extended deterrence, for using conventional or nuclear weapons against the threats posed by weapons of mass destruction, and for signaling to potential threat states the conditions under which the US might retaliate or preempt. The Department of Defense has consistently failed to deal with this issue in its policy statements since 1993. Its FY1997 budget request, and recent reports on proliferation have only talked about the counterforce aspects of counterproliferation in terms of conventional weapons.[161]

This inattention dramatizes the potential need to develop a retaliatory doctrine tailored to the defense of the Gulf. It also raises questions about the long-term regional implications of cuts in US nuclear capabilities. The US has already reduced its active nuclear stockpile by 59% since the Cold War and will reduce it by 79% by 2003. The US has also eliminated about 75% of all of its nuclear weapons storage facilities, including most forward-deployed storage sites outside the US. It has removed all tactical nuclear weapons from its ground force, taken nuclear weapons off of its carriers, removed most nuclear weapons from its tactical aircraft, and removed nuclear-armed cruise missiles from its surface ships.[162]

These are all important steps towards reducing the nuclear arms race, but their success depends on the Gulf remaining a nuclear-free zone. If Iran or Iraq should acquire nuclear weapons, the US will almost certainly be forced to extend its nuclear umbrella to the Gulf, either through its bombers or systems like its submarine-launched cruise missiles.

The Problem of Proxies, Unconventional Means, and Terrorism

Finally, much of the current discussion of counterproliferation, defenses, and extended deterrence assumes that the enemy will be a state using conventional delivery means. It is far from clear that this is the case. Iran, Iraq, or some other threat might chose to deliver weapons of mass destruction using covert means, some proxy or terrorist organization, or a commercial transport rather than a weapons system. It is impossible to explore all of the options involved in an overview of US power projection capabilities in the Gulf, but Table Sixteen provides a brief outline of the possibilities. These factors cannot be ignored in any realistic assessment of the risk posed by nuclear, chemical, and biological weapons.

TABLE SIXTEEN   The Problem of Terrorism and Unconventional Warfare

- Existing and projected detection and control technologies, arms control proposals, and concepts for missile defense assume that the primary threats are organized states and that relatively large efforts must be used.
- Conventional structures of deterrence assume identifiable and limited sets of opponents and similar values in dealing with issues like mutual destruction. Terrorist movements may be willing to take catastrophic risks, as may leaders who identify themselves with state and/or see martyrdom as a valid alternative to victory.
- War may not be between states or fought for limited strategic objectives. It may be a war of proxies or terrorists. It may be fought to destroy peoples or with minimal regard for collateral damage and risks.
- The target of unconventional uses of weapons of mass destruction may not be military in the normal sense of the term. It may be a peace process, US commitment to the defense of a given region, a peace keeping force, an election or ruling elite, or growing cooperation between formerly hostile groups.
- Terrorist organizations have already attempted to use crude chemical weapons. The development and use of chemical and biological weapons is well within the capability of many extremist and terrorist movements, and states can transfer weapons or aid such movements indirectly or with plausible deniability.
- Covert or unconventional delivery means may be preferable to both states and non-state organizations. Cargo ships, passenger aircraft, commercial vehicles, dhows, or commercial cargo shipments can all be used, and routed through multiple destinations. A well established series of covert transport and smuggling networks exist throughout the region. Biological weapons can be manufactured in situ.
- The Marine Corps Barracks incident has already shown the potential value of "mass terrorism," as had the media impact of the Oklahoma City bombing and disruptive effect of far more limited events like the suicide bombings by Hamas and the assassination of Yitzak Rabin.
- Biological weapons and chemical present special problems because they can be used in so many ways. Chemical poisons were once used to contaminate the Israeli fruit group. Infectious biological agents could be used to mirror image local diseases or with long gestation times. Persistent nerve agents could be used in subways, large buildings, shopping malls/bazaars, etc. to create both immediate casualties and long term risks. Mixes of biological and chemical agents could be used to defeat detection, protection gear or vaccines.
- Arms control efforts assume large state efforts with detectable manufacturing and weaponization programs in peacetime. The development of a capability to suddenly manufacture several hundred biological and chemical weapons with little or no warning is well within the state of the art using nothing but commercial supplies and equipment, and much of the R&D effort could be conducted as civil or defensive research.

(continues)

TABLE SIXTEEN   (*continued*)

- Unconventional and terrorist uses of weapons can involve the use of extremely high risk biological weapons transmitted by human carriers, commercial cargoes, etc.
- The incentives for the unconventional use of weapons of mass destruction increase in proportion to the lack of parity in conventional weapons, the feelings of hopelessness by alienated or extremist groups, or the prospect of catastrophic defeat.
- Similarly, the incentive for the unconventional use of weapons of mass destruction will increase in direct proportion to the perceived effectiveness of theater missile and other regular military defense systems.
- Rogue operations will be a constant temptation for state intelligence groups, militant wings of extremist groups, revolutionary forces, etc.

9

The Changing Structure of US War-Fighting Resources and Capabilities in the Gulf

It is difficult to summarize the complex and constantly changing structure of US war-fighting capabilities in the Gulf. On the one hand, the changes in US forces and strategy since Desert Storm have made significant cuts in the total pool of forces the US has available to deploy in power projection missions, and raise grave doubts about the ability of the US to fight two near simultaneous major regional contingencies. Even if one looks at the Gulf alone, it is doubtful that the US could again deploy the two corps land forces of Desert Storm. It no longer has a massive pool of heavy forces in NATO to draw upon, and the previous analysis has shown that it would take a substantial amount of time for the US to deploy even one heavy division and two and one-half months to deploy a contingency corps of three light and one heavy divisions. The US has also made major cuts in its air and naval forces which are in excess of 35%, and cuts of 45% seem likely by the year 2000. These cuts inevitably limit the forces it can deploy to the Gulf.

On the other hand, the US has scarcely ceased to be a superpower, and it faces only moderate conventional threats from Iran and Iraq. The US may have cut its air strength, but Table Seven has shown that it has reacted effectively to many of the lessons of the Gulf War and has sharply improved many aspects of the quality of its air units. The US has also improved the quality of its naval air power and the capability of naval air forces in joint warfare. It has improved many critical aspects of its C^4I capabilities, and it has begun to make major improvements in its ability to rapidly deploy heavy ground forces to the upper Gulf—one of the most critical priorities for improving US, Saudi, and Kuwaiti capabilities to deal with any new act of aggression from Iraq.

The US can draw upon powerful support from its Southern Gulf allies, and Iran and Iraq face major limitations. Iraq has rebuilt its forces since the Gulf War, but almost solely through cannibalization. It lost at least 40% of its military strength during the Gulf War, and it has not had any meaningful military resupply since mid-1990. It has had negligible access to the new weapons and technologies it needs to compensate for the deficiencies the Gulf War revealed in its land and air forces, has lost most of its small navy, and has lost virtually all of its long-range missile and chemical warfare capabilities. Its larger nuclear facilities have been destroyed, and it has at least been forced to disperse its nuclear capabilities.

The Iranian threat is more serious, but it is far from able to challenge current US capabilities. Iran has access to advanced conventional weapons, and new long-range missiles. It is producing chemical weapons, and has an extensive nuclear and biological weapons effort. Iran does not, however, have a land boundary with the Southern Gulf states and cannot easily exploit its large pool of manpower. It lost some 40% to 60% of its heavy land equipment during the final battles of the Iran-Iraq War and its navy suffered significant losses and damage during the tanker war with the US. Iran is heavily dependent on Western land, air, and naval weapons that are now 15–25 years old and which have seen extensive combat service.

Strengths in US Capabilities

The Gulf War has also shown that force numbers are not the only issue which must be considered in summarizing the trends in US military capabilities. The US enjoys major qualitative advantages over most Third World forces, particularly nations like Iran and Iraq. Table Seventeen summarizes these advantages, and they are likely to continue to give the US an important mix of "force-multipliers" in any major regional contingency in the Gulf.

It is important to note that the word "coalition" is as critical to US success as the individual qualitative advantages that US forces enjoyed over Iraq. The US cannot fight alone in the Gulf and will remain dependent on the Southern Gulf states for any mid to high-intensity air and land combat. The advantages listed in Table Seventeen are also likely to be far less significant in dealing with unconventional warfare, politically dominated low-intensity and guerrilla conflicts, urban warfare, and other specialized types of conflict, than in direct conventional combat.

TABLE SEVENTEEN   US Military Advantages in Coalition Warfare in the Gulf

- *Decoupling of political and military responsibility:* No war is ever free of command controversy or friction between political and military leadership. However, US forces fought the Gulf War with an exceptionally effective delegation of responsibility for military decisions to military commanders. The fact that this system worked was partly a matter of individual personalities, but it also reflected important changes in the way national command authority was exercised in the US in comparison with Korea and Vietnam and from the nature of coalition command in past wars.
- *Unity of command:* In spite of the formal Coalition command structure, effective unity of command took place at the level of USCINCENT. The planning and operational control of all Coalition forces, regardless of service, had a high degree of central coordination. There was no division of command by military service, or separation of operations and intelligence. National forces preserved a high degree of autonomy because they were assigned specific functions, areas, and responsibilities, but Coalition commanders supported de facto unity of command—largely due to the support that Saudi Arabia, Britain, Egypt, and France were willing to give the US. The level of unity of command, and "fusion," achieved during the Gulf War was scarcely perfect, but it was far more functional than in previous military conflicts.
- *Creation of new air battle capabilities:* Advances in aircraft, air munitions, and C4I/BM systems allowed the US to develop the capability to rapidly suppress Third World air and ground-based defense systems while simultaneously carrying out deep strategic and theater offensive strikes against both strategic and tactical targets. This gave the US the capability to initiate a major air campaign before the AirLand battle and before it defeated or suppressed enemy air capabilities and defenses.
- *Combined arms operations, joint operations, and the "AirLand Battle":* While US doctrine had always placed a pro forma emphasis on combined arms operations, many US operations in Vietnam did not properly integrate combined arms, common inter-service training in joint and combined arms operations was limited, and air operations were not properly integrated into land operations. In the years that followed, the US reorganized to place far more emphasis on combined arms and joint operations. It greatly strengthened joint operations training and career rotations into joint commands. At the same time, it developed tactics that closely integrated air and land operations into what the US came to call the "AirLand battle." These tactics were critical to the success of the ground battle.
- *Emphasis on maneuver:* The US had emphasized firepower and attrition during the end of the Vietnam War. In the years that followed, it converted its force structure to place an equal emphasis on maneuver and deception. This emphasis was supported by Britain and France, and was adopted by Saudi Arabia.
- *Emphasis on deception and strategic/tactical innovation:* No country has a monopoly on the use of deception and strategic/tactical innovation. The Coali-

(continues)

TABLE SEVENTEEN   *(continued)*

tion, however, demonstrated capabilities that were far superior to those of Iraq.

- *"24 hour war"—Superior night, all-weather, and beyond-visual-range warfare:* "Visibility" is always relative in combat. There is no such thing as a perfect night vision or all-weather combat system, or way of acquiring perfect information at long-ranges. US and British air and land forces, however, had far better training and technology for such combat than they have ever had in the past, and were the first forces designed to wage warfare continuously at night and in poor weather. Equally important, they were far more capable of taking advantage of the margin of extra range and tactical information provided by superior technology.

- *Near Real-Time Integration of C³I/BM/T/BDA:* The Coalition took advantage of major US C³I/BM/T/BDA organization, technology, and software to integrate various aspects of command, control, communications, and intelligence (C³I); battle management (BM), targeting (T), and battle damage assessment (BDA) to achieve a near real-time integration and decision-making execution cycle.

- *Integration of space warfare:* The Coalition integrated US space-based intelligence, communications, and command and control assets into its tactics and organization. This "space advantage" would have been even greater if space-based imagery had been better disseminated at the theater and tactical levels.

- *A new tempo of operations:* The Coalition exploited a superiority in every aspect of targeting, intelligence gathering and dissemination, integration of combined arms, multi-service forces, and night and all-weather warfare to achieve both a new tempo of operations and one far superior to that of Iraq.

- *A new tempo of sustainability:* The Coalition forces had maintainability, reliability, reparability, and the speed and overall mobility of logistic, service support, and combat support force activity that broadly matched their maneuver and firepower capabilities. The benefits of these new capabilities were reflected in such critical areas as the extraordinarily high operational availability and sortie rates of US aircraft, and the ability to support the movement of heliborne and armored forces during the long thrust into Iraq from the West.

- *Beyond-visual-range air combat, air defense suppression, air base attacks, and airborne C⁴I/BM:* The Coalition had a decisive advantage in air combat training, in beyond-visual-range air combat capability, in anti-radiation missiles, in electronic warfare, in air base and shelter and kill capability, in stealth and unmanned long-range strike systems, in IFF and air control capability, and in airborne C⁴I/BM systems like the E-3 and ABCCC. These advantages allowed the Coalition to win early and decisive air supremacy.

- *Focused and effective interdiction bombing:* While the Coalition's strategic bombing effort had limitations, most aspects of offensive air power were highly successful. The interdiction effort was successful in most respects. The Coalition organized effectively to use its deep-strike capabilities to carry out a rapid and effective pattern of focused strategic bombing where

(continues)

TABLE SEVENTEEN   *(continued)*

---

planning was sufficiently well coupled to intelligence and meaningful strategic objectives so that such strikes achieved the major military objectives that the planner set. At the same time, targeting, force allocation, and precision kill capabilities had advanced to the point where interdiction bombing and strikes were far more lethal and strategically useful than in previous conflicts.

- *Expansion of the battle field: "Deep Strike":* As part of its effort to offset the Warsaw Pact's superiority, US tactics and technology emphasized using air-strike and cruise-missile capabilities to extend the battlefield far beyond the immediate forward edge of the battle area (FEBA). The Coalition exploited the resulting mix of targeting capability, improved air-strike capabilities, and land-force capabilities in ways that played an important role in attriting Iraqi ground forces during the air phase of the war, and which helped the Coalition break through Iraqi defenses and exploit the breakthrough. This achievement is particularly striking in view of the fact that the US was not yet ready to employ some "deep strike" targeting technologies and precision strike systems designed to fight the Warsaw Pact that were still in development.
- *Technological superiority in many critical areas of weaponry:* The Coalition scarcely had a monopoly on effective weapons, but it had a critical edge in key weapons like tanks, other armored fighting vehicles, artillery systems, long-range strike systems, attack aircraft, air-defense aircraft, surface-to-air missiles, space, attack helicopters, naval systems, sensors, battle management and a host of other areas. As has been discussed in Chapter One, this superiority went far beyond the technical "edge" revealed by "weapon on weapon" comparisons. Coalition forces exploited technology in "systems" that integrated weapons into other aspects of force capability and into the overall force structures of the US, Britain, France, and the Saudi Air Force to a far greater degree than Iraq and most military forces in Third World states.
- *Integration of precision-guided weapons into tactics and force structures:* The Coalition exploited a decisive US technical edge in the capability of most of its precision-guided weapons over Iraq, had far more realistic training in using them, and the ability to link their employment to far superior reconnaissance and targeting capability.
- *Realistic combat training and use of technology and simulation:* The US and Britain used training methods based on realistic joint, combined arms, armored, air warfare, and AirLand training, large-scale training, and adversary training. These efforts were far superior to previous methods and were coupled to a far more realistic and demanding system for ensuring the readiness of the forces involved. Equally important, they emphasized the need for the kinds of additional training that allowed US forces to adapt to the special desert warfare conditions of Desert Storm.

(continues)

TABLE SEVENTEEN   *(continued)*

- *All volunteer military/higher entry and career standards:* British, French, US, and Saudi forces were all-volunteer professional forces. They had a decisive advantage in professional standards, training levels, and merit-based promotion.[163]
- *Emphasis on forward leadership and delegation:* Virtually all of the successful Coalition forces were aggressively led from the front. Iraqi forces were led from the rear.
- *Heavy reliance on NCOs and enlisted personnel:* There was nothing new about the heavy reliance that Western forces placed on the technical skills, leadership quality, and initiative of non-commissioned officers (NCOs) and experienced enlisted personnel. This is a reliance which is common to virtually every Western military force, and which has given them a major advantage over Soviet and those Third World forces which do not give the same authority and expertise to NCOs and career enlisted personnel. Better educated, trained, and experienced NCOs and enlisted personnel were critical to the British, French, and US ability to exploit technology, and sustain high tempo operations.
- *High degree of overall readiness:* Military readiness is a difficult term to define since it involves so many aspects of force capability. Western forces entered the Gulf War, however, with two great advantages. The first was far more realistic standards for measuring readiness and ensuring proper reporting. The second was adequate funding over a sustained period of time.
- *Clear doctrine for collateral damage:* The Coalition entered the Gulf War with explicit criteria for limiting collateral damage to Iraq's population and civilian facilities, and with the ability to prosecute the war within those limits. It avoided significant direct damage to Iraqi civilians and tailored its strikes against civil facilities to sharply reduce damage to civilian buildings, plants, and infrastructure. This proved to be an important part of shaping the political side of the battlefield.
- *Management of media relations:* While the Coalition was often criticized after the war for placing limits on the press and manipulating the information provided to the media, the fact remains that modern war is inevitably a struggle to shape media opinion. The Coalition showed superior capability to use the media access to achieve military goals.

Weaknesses in US Capabilities

At the same time, the US is scarcely "ten feet tall." Table Eighteen presents a list of potential weaknesses and vulnerabilities in US forces that could also affect the outcome of a contingency in the Gulf, and which an intelligent enemy might exploit in a future conflict. The US has already encountered such challenges in Vietnam, Beirut, Somalia, and Bosnia, and it has no guarantee that it will not encounter them in future challenges in the Gulf.

124

TABLE EIGHTEEN   Weaknesses in US Capabilities for Regional Warfare in the Gulf

- *Accepting the true politics of war:* Much of the writing on the "revolution in military affairs" still assumes that the US will only have to use military force where there is clear popular and legislative support, and tacitly assumes that any action by the US and/or its allies will have broad international support. There are two problems with this approach. The first is that the defense of strategic interests cannot always be tied to an act of naked aggression like Iraq's invasion of Kuwait. The second is that popular, legislative, and international support is always conditional and often volatile. Beginning a conflict or peace action is only the start of the political nature of war. If the enemy can exploit the political situation, there will be no contract between the military and society that will guarantee continued support.
- *Internal security and political warfare:* The US cannot rescue any Gulf government from its own people. It may help support allied internal security forces with training and technical aid, but the US position in the Gulf is ultimately dependent on the popular support available to each Gulf regime, popular perception of that regime's legitimacy, and the extent to which each Gulf government maintains a "social contract" with its people that provides them with security, jobs, and hope for the future. Most of the Southern Gulf states—excepting Bahrain, Oman, and the poorer sheikdoms of the UAE—have the oil and gas wealth to maintain relatively high current standards of income, and the wealthier Gulf states have the financial ability to help the poorer states. The question is whether the Southern Gulf states will make effective use of their wealth and be able to meet the expectations of their minorities and youth (over 40% of the population of the Southern Gulf is under 15). If Gulf governments do not deal with these problems, the US will be no more able to help them against their people than it was able to help the Shah.
- *Islamic extremism:* The US is not equipped to deal with the challenge of Islamic extremism. It can address the technical aspects of counter-terrorism and security operations, but it cannot deal with the cultural, political and religious aspects of the Islamic revival, or deal at a political level with its violent and extremist elements. Iran, Iraq, or other regional threats are almost certain to attempt to exploit the secular, Western, Christian, and pro-Israeli character of the US and to attempt to discredit the Islamic character of the Southern Gulf states. Iran is certain to exploit the Shi'ite issue as well, and Iraq to exploit its Arab identity. If the US lacks regional allies which are seen as having Islamic legitimacy, there is little the US can do to deal with the resulting politico-military problems.
- *Low-intensity realism:* Low-intensity wars are almost invariably fought in confused political circumstances against people, not things. Such wars are highly political and focus on killing rather than on destroying weapons and facilities. Western preparation for using the revolution in military affairs in peace-keeping and low-intensity conflict sometimes tacitly denies this political reality, while policy makers often commit military forces on the basis of expectations of success without fully assessing the risks. While it may be argued that the West

(continues)

has learned from Somalia, it is not clear what or how. The current peacekeeping effort in Bosnia, for example, still presents similar risks, and a characterization of Serbian, Croatian, and Muslim forces during the crisis has scarcely been a model that can support a countervailing strategy.

- *Taking casualties:* Rightly or wrongly, many potential threat nations believe that the US and other Western states face the same problem as Israel: They cannot take serious casualties in any war other than an existential threat. While such expectations may be exaggerated, efforts to exploit this weakness and produce the kind of retreat the US made from Beirut and Somalia can be taken for granted, and Western success in any future major regional contingency may be dependent on relatively quick, decisive, and low-casualty success.

- *Inflicting casualties:* The West must increasingly plan to fight at least low and mid-intensity conflicts in ways that both limit enemy casualties and show that the West is actively attempting to do so. At the same time, the "revolution in military affairs" has often avoided coming to grips with the prospect of extending combat with enemy forces where manpower is the principal target and killing people, as distinguished from things, dominates the tactical situation. The assumption is often tacitly made that the US will not engage in such fighting—an assumption that has already help lead to the US defeat in Somalia.

- *Collateral damage:* Western states will operate under growing and even more severe constraints regarding inflicting damage on enemy civilians and civilian facilities.

- *Urban and built-up area warfare:* Western military forces have never fully come to grips with the issue of urban warfare in NATO, assuming that it would either exploit largely evacuated urban/areas or could largely bypass these areas. The reluctance to fight in populated areas was at least a passing factor shaping the nature of conflict termination during the Gulf War. Western forces are not trained or equipped to deal with sustained urban warfare in populated areas in regional combat—particularly when the fighting may affect large civilian populations on friendly soil.

- *Mountain warfare and warfare in rough terrain:* Many of the systems and tactics that the Coalition exploited in the Gulf War were only possible because of the relatively flat terrain and open nature of that terrain. They would be much less decisive if better cover was available.

- *Hostage taking and terrorism:* Western governments still tend to sharply overreact to hostage taking, often making deals or concessions for political or humanitarian reasons, when long experience has shown that hostages deals almost inevitably fail. Similarly, the West still has uncertain military capabilities to deal with terrorism and unconventional warfare.

- *Sudden attack:* One of the key lessons that future threats are likely to draw from Desert Storm is the potential advantage of sudden and decisive action, and the potential value of exploiting the problems in the power projection capabilities of the US and other Western military forces. US strength may often deter war, but when deterrence fails, it is important to understand that threat powers are likely

(*continues*)

TABLE EIGHTEEN   (*continued*)

---

to escalate suddenly and stress surprise. It is equally important to understand that threat nations actively exploit reporting on shifts in US defense spending and force levels, and will focus on the problems in Western power projection capabilities revealed in budget documents, legislative debates and the media.

- *Extended deterrence and battles of intimidation:* At present, the US is better prepared for war-fighting than it is in defining a clear structure of regional deterrence based on exploiting the weaknesses of threat nations, and reassuring and strengthening allies. Many crises and regional issues, however, are decided by "no intensity" conflict. They are the product of whether one nation can intimidate another, often to win limited victories that do not threaten the survival or ruling elite in neighboring states. The current Iranian build-up in the Gulf seems to have this focus. So do some aspects of North Korea's manipulation of its nuclear threat, (or threat of acquiring nuclear capability), and the Chinese build-up of capabilities that may affect decisions on control of the South China Sea. The problem the US faces in countering such pressures and in extending deterrence to a regional level is one that it is only beginning to address.

- *Weapons of mass destruction:* The Coalition emerged from Desert Storm claiming a victory over Iraq in destroying its weapons of mass destruction that it never achieved. It had firmly identified only two of 21 major Iraqi nuclear facilities before the war, struck only 8 by the time the war ended, did not properly characterize the functions of more than half the facilities it struck, and never completed effective BDA. Coalition strikes on Iraqi chemical facilities left 150,000 munitions intact—most of which suffered far more from design defects than Coalition attacks. Iraq's biological warfare capabilities seemed to have been evacuated, and remain largely intact. The Coalition "Scud Hunt" failed and never produced a confirmed kill. Future wars are certain to present far more serious and time urgent threats, and involve far more developed planning to try to exploit possession of such weapons.

- *Ecological and environmental warfare; water and infrastructure warfare:* The burning oil fields and oil spills of the Gulf War did not materially affect the ecology of Kuwait and the Gulf. They did, however, set a precedent for environmental warfare that may be more important in the future. There is often only a narrow line between military actions that affect the environment, and actions that affect key aspects of human survival like attacks on water facilities and power facilities that affect key human services and attacks on fuel facilities. Weapons of mass destruction are not the only way of achieving large-scale damage or high civilian casualties.

- *Limits of UN/cooperative/coalition warfare:* As the Kurdish crisis of September 1996 demonstrated, allied states often have different strategic interests and perceptions from the US. Key allies like France, Turkey, and Saudi Arabia may differ with the US over the need to take military action and the nature of the action to be taken. Most Southern Gulf and other Arab states now differ from the US on many aspects of its security policy towards Iran and Iraq, and the election of the Likud government in Israel has made them even more sensitive to the pres-

---

(*continues*)

TABLE EIGHTEEN   (*continued*)

ence of US forces on their territory. While coalition warfare offers many potential advantages, it also confronts the US with the practical problem of understanding the strengths and weaknesses of potential and actual allied nations and forces, and integrating them into the "revolution in military affairs." Even when allied nations fully support US action, coalitions are difficult to transform into effective war fighting capabilities. Britain, France, and the US deployed to Saudi Arabia in Desert Storm under conditions where it took several months to realistically assess Saudi forces and begin efforts to develop more interoperable war-fighting capabilities. The fact that Egypt and Syria were reluctant to execute an offensive into Kuwait came as a surprise to USCINCENT, although this should scarcely have been a surprise in the case of Syria.

- *Extended conflict and occupation warfare:* Not all wars can be quickly terminated, and many forms of warfare—particularly those involving peace-keeping and peace-enforcement—require prolonged military occupations. Western states, and certainly the US, are increasingly reluctant to engage in extended conflict at any level of warfare, and have shown little interest in prolonged military occupations and in dealing with the politico-military aftermath of conflict and peacekeeping exercises.

There is no way to predict which of these weaknesses, if any, will be exploited in a future crisis or conflict, or how they will compare to the strengths the US can bring to bear. It is important to note, however, that many of the potential weaknesses listed in Table Eighteen are only weaknesses if the Southern Gulf states falter in dealing with their own internal problems, divide against each other, or fail to cooperate with the US early enough to create an effective structure of deterrence.

The US will not be able to effectively project power in the Gulf, or exploit the potential advantages listed in Table Seventeen, if it is not sensitive to their differing strategic views and internal problems, and if it does not work closely with the Southern Gulf states, encourage collective regional security through organizations like the Gulf Cooperation Council, maintain the combat ready US forces needed for effective power projection, invest in the kind of modernization necessary to maintain its technical edge, and develop effective counterproliferation capabilities. The US-led victory in the Gulf War is no insurance for the future, and the US will only be a strong as its defense budgets, force levels, and ties to its allies permit.

The Need for Strategic Commitment

It is easy to oversimplify the situation and to deal with US capabilities in terms of dire warnings or exaggerated complaisance. In reality, however, the trends in US military capabilities in the Gulf are highly complex and are often contradictory. As a result, the problem in reaching any conclusions about US capabilities is to decide whether the cup is half-empty or half-full.

The US has many strategic and military strengths in the region, which combine with the strengths of its Southern Gulf allies:

- The lack of any major outside opponent: a legacy of the end of the Cold War.
- The Coalition victory in the Gulf War.
- A decisive US and allied superiority in the Gulf region in many areas of deployed military technology.
- Southern Gulf allies which offer the US more support than at any time in the past, and which are capable of both aiding US rapid rein-forcement and sustaining many aspects of US power.
- Relatively robust world oil export capabilities.
- Improvements in US power projection capabilities in many of the areas exposed as problems during the Gulf War—including upgrad-ing the strike capabilities of US fighters, improved prepositioning, improved sealift, and improved readiness and force management for US Army forces.
- A current ability to win control of the seas in the Gulf and achieve air superiority rapidly.
- UN sanctions which have destroyed most of Iraq's capability to use and produce weapons of mass destruction, coupled to half a decade in which Iraq has been cut off from major arms imports.
- An Iran that lost 40% or more of its ground force equipment in 1988, and which is still heavily dependent on US and British supplied equipment that is now worn and largely obsolete—with ages of 15 to 25 years without MSIPs or comprehensive renovation. An impov-erished Iran has also had to cut back sharply on its arms imports since the Gulf War, and so far is only making slow progress in acquiring nuclear weapons.
- Time in which to help build-up Southern Gulf forces, complete efforts to improve US power projection capabilities, and develop counterproliferation capabilities, because of the inevitable delays in any Iranian and Iraqi military build-up.

At the same time, the US faces a number of problems and future chal-lenges in dealing with Iran and Iraq, Southern Gulf states, and the impact of declining US defense budgets:

- The probability that Iraq will remain a revanchist and authoritarian state, the possibility of a backlash against US policy, and the probabil-ity that Iraqi will break out from the UN sanctions before the year 2000.

- Growing problems with the Kurdish security zone and infighting between the Kurds of Talabani and Barzani.
- Near isolation in pursuing a policy of "dual containment" towards Iran, with little or no practical support—even in the region—for the economic and political isolation of Iran.
- Problems in establishing US credibility regarding claims about the Iranian threat—including recent US charges about Iranian deployment of chemical weapons on islands in the Gulf, the volume of Iranian arms sales, and the role of Rafsanjani and the Iranian ruling elite in terrorism.[164]
- The risk of a sudden "breakout" in Iranian or Iraqi nuclear capabilities if either state should be able to buy fissile material from the former Soviet Union or any other suppliers, or "breakout" in deploying advanced biological weapons.
- The failure of the Gulf Cooperation Council to emerge as a cohesive military alliance.
- Continuing waste and lack of integration in most Southern Gulf military purchasing efforts and the slow development of integrated air, maritime surveillance, and anti-mine capabilities.
- Tensions between the friendly Southern Gulf states: Saudi vs. Oman, Bahrain vs. Qatar, Qatar vs. Saudi, divisions in UAE, old tensions with Kuwait.
- Growing uncertainties within the Southern Gulf states regarding US forces and commitments, and the impact of US budget and force cuts on US capabilities in the Gulf.
- Growing economic and ethnic problems in many Southern Gulf states, coupled to the problem of Islamist extremism.
- A lack of full coordination with the Southern Gulf states in prepositioning US land forces equipment, and dealing with the problem of counter-terrorism.
- US attitudes and politics that exacerbate the Western tendency to confuse the Islamic revival with Islamist extremism, and make the "clash of civilizations" a self-fulfilling prophecy.
- The lack of clear force plans and contingency plans to deal with the problem of counterproliferation.
- A lack of a clear long-term US policy for dealing with energy emergencies, coupled to weak US and GCC modeling of energy vulnerabilities and trends in the Gulf region.

It is highly unlikely that the US can "fill the cup." In fact, it is virtually certain that the real test of US capabilities will be the willingness to engage in an enduring struggle to keep the cup at least two-thirds full. The US certainly has the present and planned military resources to do so if it only faces a major commitment in the Gulf, particularly if it receives continuing support from its Southern Gulf allies. At the same time, there is no simple solution to the problem of maintaining US capabilities in the region, and there is no way to make further major savings in US forces or in related US defense spending. The US must clearly recognize that it has a long-term strategic commitment in the Gulf, and must be willing to engage in a constant effort to deal with each of the problems and uncertainties raised in this analysis.

At some point, the President, the Congress, and the American people must also decide whether they are willing to spend what it takes to maintain the present commitment and superpower status of the US. The US strategic debate often concentrates on the search for new strategies, new technologies and new force mixes that can somehow allow the US to do more militarily with less manpower, fewer forces, and smaller defense budgets. There is good reason to suspect, however, that such debate is largely illusory. The last quarter century has been filled with attempts to make the US defense establishment more efficient, and none have changed the basic ratio of the cost of US military capabilities relative to US military commitments. Ultimately, the choice may boil down to one of whether the US is willing to devote at least 3% of its GNP, or around $400 billion a year, to maintain its military forces. At least in the mid term, it is unlikely to be able to spend less without accepting growing military risks in Southwest Asia and the rest of the world.

Notes

Chapter 1

1. International Energy Agency (IEA), *Middle East Oil and Gas*, Paris, IEA, OECD, 1995, p. 25; *Oil and Gas Journal*, December 26, 1994.

2. For typical estimates of world energy balances and dependence on Gulf oil and gas, see Department of Energy (DOE)/Energy Information Agency (EIA), *International Energy Outlook, 1995*, Washington, DOE/EIA, June 1995; International Energy Agency (IEA), *World Energy Outlook*, Paris, IEA, 1995. IEA and DOE do not provide country breakouts for Bahrain and Oman. Reserve data estimated by author based on country data

3. Calculated in constant FY1995 dollars, budget authority for the Department of Defense are planned to drop to a low of $242.8 billion in FY1997, and budget obligations are planned to drop to a low of $244.2 billion in FY1998. Total budget authority for defense is planned to drop to a low of $253.4 billion in FY1997, and budget obligations are planned to drop to a low of $254.5 billion in FY1998. Lt. General Richard L. West, "The 1996 DoD Budget: Outlook for the Army," *Army*, April 1995, p. 29.

Chapter 2

4. The US fiscal years begins on October 1st. US defense expenditures can be reported in a number of ways. Some totals only count the money spent by the Department of Defense, but most figures on total defense spending include additional money spent by the Department of Energy. In addition to Budget Authority, defense spending can be counted in terms of Budget Outlays, which only includes the money to be spent in a given fiscal year, and not money authorized for future years. Neither figure measures the actual cash flow out the Treasury within a given fiscal year, which is a mix of funds provided in the authorizations of past years and current outlays.

5. Secretary of Defense William J. Perry, *Annual Report to the President and the Congress*, Department of Defense, Washington, February, 1995, pp. 272–273; Department of Defense Press Release No. 106-96, March 4, 1996.

6. Secretary of Defense William J. Perry, *Annual Report to the President and the Congress*, Department of Defense, Washington, February, 1995, p. B-3; Department of Defense Press Release No. 106-96, March 4, 1996.

7. FY1996 DoD Budget Briefing, Secretary of Defense, February 6, 1995.

8. Secretary of Defense William J. Perry, *Annual Report to the President and the Congress*, Department of Defense, Washington, February, 1995, pp. 271–273; Department of Defense Press Release No. 106-96, March 4, 1996.

9. Secretary of Defense William J. Perry, *Annual Report to the President and the Congress*, Department of Defense, Washington, February, 1995, pp. 272–273.

10. Source: *US Federal Budget, FY1997*, p. 167. The projected trends for the Department of Defense alone show an increase budget authority in current dollars from an actual spending level of $255.7 billion in FY1995 to $251.8 billion in FY1996, $242.6 billion in FY1997, $248.1 billion in FY1998, $254.3 billion in FY1999, $261.7 billion in FY2000, $269.6 billion in FY2001, and $276.6 billion in FY2002.

11. Source: *US Federal Budget, FY1997*, p. 166. The projected trends for the Department of Defense alone show an increase budget outlays in current dollars from an actual spending level of $259.4 billion in FY1995 to $254.3 billion in FY1996, $247.5 billion in FY1997, $243.9 billion in FY1998, $246.5 billion in FY1999, $253.9 billion in FY2000, $256.6 billion in FY2001, and $264.9 billion in FY2002.

12. Secretary of Defense's presentation aids to Congress for the FY1996 budget submission, February, 1996.

13. Source: *US Federal Budget, FY1997*, pp. 166–167.

14. *Defense News*, March 4, 1996, p. 37.

15. David Silverberg, "Predictions, Predictions . . . ," *Armed Forces Journal*, January, 1996, p. 13; *Defense News*, March 4, 1996, p. 37.

16. *Defense News*, March 4, 1996, p. 37.

17. *Jane's Defense Weekly*, January 31, 1996, p. 5, February 21, 1996; *Defense Week*, March 4, 1996, p. 1, March 11, 1996, pp. 14–23.

18. *Defense News*, October 16–22, 1995, pp. 1, 48, 92. For more detailed analysis, see CSIS, *The Defense Train Wreck*, Washington, CSIS, 1995 and Harlan K. Ullman, *In Irons: US Military Might in the New Century*, Washington, National Defense University, 1995.

19. *Defense News*, October 16–22, 1995, pp. 1, 48, 92. For more detailed analysis, see CSIS, *The Defense Train Wreck*, Washington, CSIS, 1995 and Harlan K. Ullman, *In Irons: US Military Might in the New Century*, Washington, National Defense University, 1995.

20. Secretary Perry has indicated that that the Army needs at least $1 billion more for its FY1996 $6.3 billion modernization budget. *Jane's Defense Weekly*, August 5, 1995, p. 21; *Los Angeles Times*, May 31, 1995, p. 1.

21. US Department of Defense budget briefing; Statement of William J. Perry before the Senate Budgeting Committee, February 10, 1995.

22. Secretary of Defense's presentation aids to Congress for the FY1996 budget submission, February, 1996.

23. *Defense News*, January 29, 1996, p. 4.

24. *Defense News*, January 8, 1996, p. 29.

25. *Defense News*, January 29, 1996, p. 22.

26. Based upon a detailed program comparison in each program area. The reader should be aware that specific system or project funding details for the FYDP and weapons procurement documents are classified and cannot be addressed in this analysis. Also see *Defense Daily*, May 31, 1995, p. 305 and *Defense News*, July 3–9, 1995, p. 4.

27. *Defense News*, April 29, 1996, p. 29, May 6, 1996, p. 6.

28. *Defense News*, March 11, 1996, p. 22.

29. *Defense News*, May 22, 1995, p. 30; May 29, 1995, p. 4; *Army*, June 1995, p. 8, September, 1995, p. 10; *Jane's Defense Weekly*, June 3, 1995, p. 4, August 5, 1995, pp. 21–22; *Los Angeles Times*, May 31, 1995, p. 1

30. Statement by General John M. Shalikashvili, Chairman of the Joint Chiefs of Staff, before the Budget Committee of the US Senate, February 10, 1995, p. 20.

31. See, for example, the warnings of Brigadier General Johnny Riggs (Director of Requirements in the US Army's office of the Deputy Chief of Staff for Operation) that underfunding could increase US casualties by up to 11,000 in a future war, and by Lt. General Ronald Hite that US Army modernization funding was too low to fund essential programs at an efficient rate. *Defense News*, October 16, 1995, p. 48.

Chapter 3

32. Base Force briefing aids issued by the Department of Defense in August, 1990, and supplementary briefing aids issued by the Office of the Joint Chiefs of Staff in February, 1991 and February, 1992 as part of the presentation of the FY1992 and FY1993 defense budgets to Congress.

33. Clinton Campaign information sheets, October, 1992.

34. The OMB data did not always track in detail with the data in Vision of Change for America, but are considered to be more authoritative by the White House staff. Such differences are normal because of the different publication dates of such material. The latest document usually contains the more authoritative corrections.

35. This emphasis on cutting defense followed the pattern set by the Budget Summit agreement that President Bush had reached with senior Democrats in the Congress in the fall of 1990. Under this budget agreement, defense was the only part of the federal budget that was to take its fair share of cuts during the coming five years. Increases took place in entitlement spending and discretionary domestic spending, and transformed the supposed $500 billion cut in the budget deficit into a massive real world increase. In contrast, defense spending was cut more than was called for by the Budget Summit.

36. Estimates included in background briefing by the staff of the Senate Appropriations Committee.

37. Figures are taken from briefing aids circulated by the Office of Defense in March, 1993

38. Figures are taken from briefing aids circulated by the Office of Defense in March 1993.

Chapter 4

39. Based on the text provided by Secretary of Defense Aspin to the House and Senate Armed Services Committees in presenting the results of the Bottom Up Review in September 1993.

40. The reader should be aware that this description of the four phases of combat is adapted from three different sets of briefing aids issued by Secretary Aspin between September 1, 1993 and September 7, 1993, but largely quotes or paraphrases the narrative text in the pamphlet version of these briefing aids.

41. Ibid.

42. Based on a combination of the tables and text provided by Secretary of Defense Aspin to the House and Senate Armed Services Committees in presenting the results of the Bottom Up Review in September, 1993. Although dated September 1, 1993, several tables were revised, added, or deleted during September 1st through September 14th.

43. Estimate based on the figures in the relevant country chapter in IISS, *Military Balance, 1995–1996*, London, IISS, 1995.

44. Estimate based on the figures in the relevant country chapter in IISS, *Military Balance, 1994–1995*, London, IISS, 1994.

45. Estimate based on the figures in the relevant country chapter in IISS, *Military Balance, 1995–1996*, London, IISS, 1995.

46. Based on a combination of the tables and text provided by Secretary of Defense Aspin to the House and Senate Armed Services Committees in presenting the results of the Bottom Up Review in September, 1993. Although dated September 1, 1993, several tables were revised, added, or deleted during September 1st through September 14th.

Chapter 5

47. Ibid.

48. No agreement was reached over specific program details. Bureaucratic and inter-service fights over the structure and future funding of theater defense programs continue at this writing.

49. Data provided by the US Army staff, November, 1994.

50. Data provided by the US Navy and USMC staff, December, 1994.

51. Data provided by the US Air Force staff, December, 1994.

52. The unclassified portions of the Department of Defense data base for the Conduct of the War or "COW" study reveal many cases where the US used more than 50% of its inventory of special purpose equipment, weapons systems, and stocks for the Gulf War. For example, the US Army used more than 76% of many of its world-wide stocks of key types of logistic vehicles in spite of massive assistance from host countries, and Japanese aid in providing civilian vehicles.

53. *Washington Post*, November, 18, 1995, p. A-1.

54. Interviews.

55. *Jane's Defense Weekly*, May 27, 1995, p. 11; *Washington Times*, July 4, 1995, p. 3; Reuters, September 4, 1995, 0617.

56. *Defense News*, January 8, 1996, p. 4.

57. *Jane's Defense Weekly*, June 10, 1995, p. 63; December 9, 1995, p. 8.

58. Reuters, September 4, 1995, 0617.

59. Reuters, March 24, 1996, 0926.

60. *Jane's Defense Weekly*, April 10, 1996, p. 8.

61. *Defense News*, April 1, 1997, p. 18.

62. Interviews and *Defense News*, September 25, 1995, p. 10.

63. US Army briefing sheets, 1994.

64. *Army*, October 1994, p. 189–191; *Armed Forces Journal*, August 1995, pp. 28–30.

65. *Armed Forces Journal*, August 1995, pp. 28–30; Dennis Steele, "Roles and Missions Report," *Army*, July 1995, pp. 9–10.

66. Reuters, March 11, 1996, 1243 and March 18, 1996, 1216; *The Estimate*, March 15, 1996, p. 4.

67. US MSC briefing, January 1995.

68. US MSC briefing, January 1995.

69. US MSC briefing, January 1995.

70. *Jane's Defense Weekly*, May 27, 1995, p. 16.

71. Secretary of Defense William J. Perry, *Annual Report to the President and the Congress*, Department of Defense, Washington, February 1995, pp. 219–220.

72. USAF briefings and briefing sheets, December 1994; *Air Force Times*, December 19, 1994, p. 22.

73. Interviews, *Defense News*, April 1, 1996, p. 30.

74. Interviews, *Defense News*, March 4, 1996, pp. 8–9.

75. *Jane's Defense Weekly*, January 24, 1996, p. 6; *Defense News*, March 4, 1996, pp. 8–14; see Steven M. Kosiak, "Challenges & Opportunities: US Nonproliferation and Counterproliferation Programs in 1996," Washington, Center for Strategic and Budgetary Assessments, February 1996, pp. 31–36.

76. *Armed Forces Journal*, June 1995, p. 46.

77. *Defense News*, September 25, 1995, p. 4.

78. Interviews, DoD FY1997 budget request, *Defense News*, February 5, 1996, p. 10.

79. For a good overview and survey of the literature on this subject, see Steven M. Kosiak, "Challenges & Opportunities: US Nonproliferation and Counterproliferation Programs in 1996," Washington, Center for Strategic and Budgetary Assessments, February 1996, pp. 25–30. Also see *Defense News*, March 11, 1996, p. 20.

80. Interviews, Steven M. Kosiak, "Challenges & Opportunities: US Nonproliferation and Counterproliferation Programs in 1996," Washington, Center for Strategic and Budgetary Assessments, February, 1996, pp. 19–24; *Jane's Defense Weekly*, January 10, 1996, p. 6.

81. *Jane's Defense Weekly*, January 31, 1996, p. 5, February 21, 1996; *Defense Week*, March 4, 1996, p. 1, March 11, 1996, pp. 14–23.

82. See Eliot A. Cohen, *Gulf War Air Power Survey: Volume II, Part II*, pp. 106–107. Note that the definition of these figures differs somewhat from similar data used in Chapter Three.

Chapter 6

83. Statement of General J. H. Binford Peay III, Commander in Chief, US Central Command, before the Senate Armed Services Committee, February, 14, 1995.

84. The US Senate approved this agreement on June 29, 1972. Dale Bruner, "US Military and Security Relations with the Southern Gulf States," Washington, NSSP, Georgetown University, May 8, 1995; Michael A. Palmer, *Guardians of the Gulf: A History of America's Expending Role in the Persian Gulf, 1833–1992*, New York, The Free Press, 1992, p. 93.

85. Dale Bruner, "US Military and Security Relations with the Southern Gulf States," Washington, NSSP, Georgetown University, May 8, 1995; Michael A. Palmer, *Guardians of the Gulf: A History of America's Expending Role in the Persian Gulf, 1833–1992*, New York, The Free Press, 1992, p. 93.

86. Interviews in Bahrain in March, 1991. Saudi MODA briefing aid, March, 1991. Cohen, Dr. Eliot A, Director, *Gulf War Air Power Survey, Volume V*, Washington, US Air Force/Government Printing Office, 1993, pp. 232–233, 319, 338, 340.

87. Deutsche Press-Agentur, October 19, 1994.

88. *Jane's Defense Weekly*, November 4, 1995, p. 25.

89. Defense Security Assistance Agency (DSAA), Foreign Military Sales, *Foreign Military Construction Sales, and Military Assistance Facts As of September 30, 1993*, Washington, DC; FMS Control and Reports Division, Comptroller, DSAA, 1994, pp. 2–3, 16–17.

90. Defense Security Assistance Agency (DSAA), Foreign Military Sales, *Foreign Military Construction Sales, and Military Assistance Facts As of September 30, 1993*, Washington, DC; FMS Control and Reports Division, Comptroller, DSAA, 1994, pp. 2–3, 16–17. Covers FY1991–FY1993.

91. Defense Security Assistance Agency (DSAA), Foreign Military Sales, *Foreign Military Construction Sales, and Military Assistance Facts As of September 30, 1993*, Washington, DC; FMS Control and Reports Division, Comptroller, DSAA, 1994, pp. 94–95, 102–103.

92. Stephen Dagget and Gary J. Pagliano, "Persian Gulf War: US Costs and Allied Financial Contributions," Congressional Research Service IB91019, September, 21, 1992, pp. 11–13.

93. Rosemary Hollis, *Gulf Security: No Consensus*, London, RUSI, 1993.

94. Dale Bruner, "US Military and Security Relations with the Southern Gulf States," Washington, NSSP, Georgetown University, May 8, 1995.

95. Defense Security Assistance Agency (DSAA), Foreign Military Sales, *Foreign Military Construction Sales, and Military Assistance Facts As of September 30, 1993*, Washington, DC; FMS Control and Reports Division, Comptroller, DSAA, 1994, pp. 2–3, 16–17. Covers FY1991–FY1993.

96. Defense Security Assistance Agency (DSAA), Foreign Military Sales, *Foreign Military Construction Sales, and Military Assistance Facts As of September 30, 1993*, Washington, DC; FMS Control and Reports Division, Comptroller, DSAA, 1994, pp. 2–3, 16–17.

97. Dale Bruner, "US Military and Security Relations with the Southern Gulf States," Washington, NSSP, Georgetown University, May 8, 1995.

98. Defense Security Assistance Agency (DSAA), Foreign Military Sales, *Foreign Military Construction Sales, and Military Assistance Facts As of September 30, 1993*, Washington, DC; FMS Control and Reports Division, Comptroller, DSAA, 1994, pp. 10–11.

99. Dale Bruner, "US Military and Security Relations with the Southern Gulf States," Washington, NSSP, Georgetown University, May 8, 1995; Michael A. Palmer, *Guardians of the Gulf: A History of America's Expending Role in the Persian Gulf, 1833–1992*, New York, The Free Press, 1992, p. 93.

100. Deutsche Press-Agentur, October 19, 1994.

101. Defense Security Assistance Agency (DSAA), Foreign Military Sales, *Foreign Military Construction Sales, and Military Assistance Facts As of September 30, 1993*, Washington, DC; FMS Control and Reports Division, Comptroller, DSAA, 1994, pp. 2–3, 16–17.

102. Defense Security Assistance Agency (DSAA), Foreign Military Sales, *Foreign Military Construction Sales, and Military Assistance Facts As of September 30, 1993*, Washington, DC; FMS Control and Reports Division, Comptroller, DSAA, 1994, pp. 2–3, 16–17. Covers FY1991–FY1993.

103. Defense Security Assistance Agency (DSAA), Foreign Military Sales, *Foreign Military Construction Sales, and Military Assistance Facts As of September 30, 1993*, Washington, DC; FMS Control and Reports Division, Comptroller, DSAA, 1994, pp. 94–95, 102–103.

104. Saudi MODA briefing aid, March, 1991. Cohen, Dr. Eliot A, Director, *Gulf War Air Power Survey, Volume V*, Washington, US Air Force/Government Printing Office, 1993, pp. 232–233, 304–305, 317, 319, 329, 401.

105. *Washington Times*, March 24, 1995, p. 15; David C. Morrison, "Gathering Storm," *National Journal*, August 20, 1994, p. 1963.

106. Defense Security Assistance Agency (DSAA), Foreign Military Sales, *Foreign Military Construction Sales, and Military Assistance Facts As of September 30, 1993*, Washington, DC; FMS Control and Reports Division, Comptroller, DSAA, 1994, pp. 2–3, 16–17.

107. Defense Security Assistance Agency (DSAA), Foreign Military Sales, *Foreign Military Construction Sales, and Military Assistance Facts As of September 30, 1993*, Washington, DC; FMS Control and Reports Division, Comptroller, DSAA, 1994, pp. 2–3, 16–17. Covers FY1991–FY1993.

108. Gulshan Dietl, *Through Two Wars and Beyond: A Study of the Gulf Cooperation Council*, New Delhi, Lancers Books, 1991, p. 140.

109. Defense Security Assistance Agency (DSAA), Foreign Military Sales, *Foreign Military Construction Sales, and Military Assistance Facts As of September 30, 1993*, Washington, DC; FMS Control and Reports Division, Comptroller, DSAA, 1994, pp. 10–11.

110. Stephen Dagget and Gary J. Pagliano, "Persian Gulf War: US Costs and Allied Financial Contributions," Congressional Research Service IB91019, September, 21, 1992, pp. 11–13.

111. Rosemary Hollis, *Gulf Security: No Consensus*, London, RUSI, 1993.

112. Interview with Prince Khalid bin Sultan., March 1991.

113. Interview with senior Saudi official, November 1993.

114. Cohen, Dr. Eliot A, Director, *Gulf War Air Power Survey, Volume V*, Washington, US Air Force/Government Printing Office, 1993, pp. 232 and 279–287. Note that these data are not consistent from table to table.

115. Cohen, Dr. Eliot A, Director, *Gulf War Air Power Survey, Volume V*, Washington, US Air Force/Government Printing Office, 1993, pp. 316–317, 335, 340, 343, 641, 653–654.

116. Dale Bruner, "US Military and Security Relations with the Southern Gulf States," Washington, NSSP, Georgetown University, May 8, 1995.

117. Defense Security Assistance Agency (DSAA), Foreign Military Sales, *Foreign Military Construction Sales, and Military Assistance Facts As of September 30, 1993*, Washington, DC, pp. 10–11.

118. Defense Security Assistance Agency (DSAA), Foreign Military Sales, *Foreign Military Construction Sales, and Military Assistance Facts As of September 30, 1993*, Washington, DC; FMS Control and Reports Division, Comptroller, DSAA, 1994, pp. 2–3, 16–17. Covers FY1991–FY1993.

119. Defense Security Assistance Agency (DSAA), Foreign Military Sales, *Foreign Military Construction Sales, and Military Assistance Facts As of September 30, 1993*, Washington, DC; FMS Control and Reports Division, Comptroller, DSAA, 1994, pp. 2–3, 16–17.

120. Stephen Dagget and Gary J. Pagliano, "Persian Gulf War: US Costs and Allied Financial Contributions," Congressional Research Service IB91019, September, 21, 1992, pp. 11–13.

121. Saudi MODA briefing aid, March, 1991. Cohen, Dr. Eliot A, Director, *Gulf War Air Power Survey, Volume V*, Washington, US Air Force/Government Printing Office, 1993, p. 232–233, 304–305, 317, 401.

122. Deutsche Press-Agentur, October 19, 1994.

123. Defense Security Assistance Agency (DSAA), Foreign Military Sales, *Foreign Military Construction Sales, and Military Assistance Facts As of September 30, 1993*, Washington, DC; FMS Control and Reports Division, Comptroller, DSAA, 1994, pp. 2–3, 16–17. Covers FY1991–FY1993.

124. Defense Security Assistance Agency (DSAA), Foreign Military Sales, *Foreign Military Construction Sales, and Military Assistance Facts As of September 30, 1993*, Washington, DC; FMS Control and Reports Division, Comptroller, DSAA, 1994, pp. 2–3, 16–17.

125. *Washington Times*, August 29, 1995; *Jane's Defense Weekly*, August 26, 1995, p. 3.

126. *New York Times*, January 30, 1996, p. A-6.

127. *Jane's Defense Weekly*, July 22, 1995, p. 19; *New York Times*, January 30, 1996, p. A-6.

128. Office of the Secretary of Defense, *United States Security Strategy for the Middle East*, Washington, Department of Defense, 1995, p. 13.

129. *Jane's Defense Weekly*, July 22, 1995, p. 19.

130. Statement of General J. H. Binford Peay III, Commander in Chief, US Central Command, before the Senate Armed Services Committee, February, 14, 1995; Secretary of Defense William J. Perry, *Annual Report to the President and the Congress*, Department of Defense, Washington, February 1995, pp. 34–36.

131. *Jane's Defense Weekly*, July 22, 1995, p. 19.

132. *Jane's Defense Week*, February 25, 1995, p. 8.

133. US Army briefing, October 1994; Secretary of Defense William J. Perry, *Annual Report to the President and the Congress*, Department of Defense, Washington, February 1995, pp. 34–36.

134. Reuters, November 4, 1995, 1022.

Chapter 7

135. *Jane's Defense Weekly*, August 19, 1995, p. 6.

136. General J. H. Binford Peay III, *United States Central Command, Posture Statement, FY1995*, March 1994, pp. 42–44.

137. General J. H. Binford Peay III, *United States Central Command, Posture Statement, FY1995*, March 1994, pp. 42–44.

138. General J. H. Binford Peay III, *United States Central Command, Posture Statement, FY1995*, March 1994, pp. 42–44.

Chapter 8

139. Secretary of Defense William J. Perry, *Annual Report to the President and the Congress*, Department of Defense, Washington, February 1995, p. 71.

140. Leonard S. Spector, Mark G. McDonough, and Evan S. Medeiros, *Tracking Nuclear Proliferation*, Washington, Carnegie Endowment, 1995, pp. 119–123.

141. *Washington Post*, May 17, 1995, p. A-23; *New York Times*, May 19, 1995, p. A-1; Leonard S. Spector, Mark G. McDonough, and Evan S. Medeiros, *Tracking Nuclear Proliferation*, Washington, Carnegie Endowment, 1995, pp. 119–123.

142. Leonard S. Spector, Mark G. McDonough, and Evan S. Medeiros, *Tracking Nuclear Proliferation*, Washington, Carnegie Endowment, 1995, pp. 119–123.

143. *New York Times*, February 23, 1995, May 18, 1995, p. A-11; *Washington Post*, May 8, 1995, p. A-22; *Nucleonics Week*, February 13, 1992, p. 12, October 14, 1993, p. 9, December 16, 1993, p. 11, September 22, 1994, p. 1, October 6, 1994, p. 11; *Washington Post*, February 14, 1992, February 12, 1995; *Nuclear Fuel*, March 14, 1994, p. 9, March 28, 1994, p. 10; *Nuclear Engineering*, April 1992, p. 67, November, 1994, pp. 4, 10, UPI, November 21, 1994, Reuters, November 20, 1994.

144. According to one report by Zalmay Khalizad in *Survival*, Pakistan was deeply involved in this $10 billion effort, as was China. US experts do not confirm these reports. *Washington Post*, May 17, 1995, p. A-23.

145. *Washington Times*, May 17, 1995, p. A-15.

146. See Anthony H. Cordesman and Abraham R. Wagner, *The Lessons of Modern War, Volume IV*, Boulder, Westview, 1995, Chapter 11; Dr. Andrew Rathmell, "Iraq—The Endgame?" *Jane's Intelligence Review*, Volume 7, Number 5, pp. 224–228; and Leonard S. Spector, Mark G. McDonough, and Evan S. Medeiros, *Tracking Nuclear Proliferation*, Washington, Carnegie Endowment, 1995, pp. 119–123

147. *Jane's Defense Weekly*, May 13, 1995, p. 5.

148. *Defense News*, August 28, 1995, p. 1.

149. *Defense News*, September 25, 1996, p. 4.

150. Secretary of Defense William J. Perry, *Annual Report to the President and the Congress, FY1996*, Department of Defense, Washington, February 1995, pp. 73–76; and *Annual Report to the President and the Congress, FY1997*, Department of Defense, Washington, February 1996, pp. 53–62, 84–86. 219–224.

151. Secretary of Defense William J. Perry, *Annual Report to the President and the Congress, FY1996*, Department of Defense, Washington, February 1995, pp. 73–76; and *Annual Report to the President and the Congress, FY1997*, Department of Defense, Washington, February 1996, pp. 53–62, 84–86. 219–224; Office of the Secretary of Defense, *Proliferation: Threat and Response*, Washington, Department of Defense, April 1996, pp. 47–62 and Annex A.

152. Office of the Secretary of Defense, *Proliferation: Threat and Response*, Washington, Department of Defense, April 1996, pp. 47–62 and Annex A; Secretary of Defense William J. Perry, *Annual Report to the President and the Congress, FY1996*, Department of Defense, Washington, February 1995, pp. 73–76; and *Annual Report to the President and the Congress, FY1997*, Department of Defense, Washington, February 1996, pp. 53–62, 84–86. 219–224.

153. Office of the Secretary of Defense, *Proliferation: Threat and Response*, Washington, Department of Defense, April 1996, pp. 47–62 and Annex A; Secretary of Defense William J. Perry, *Annual Report to the President and the Congress, FY1997*, Department of Defense, Washington, February 1996, pp. 56–57; *Defense News*, November 6, 1995, p. 20.

154. *Defense News*, November 6, 1995, p. 20.

155. *Army*, July 1995, pp. 18–22.

156. *Defense News*, October 30, 1995, p. 22.

157. Ballistic Missile Defense Office, *Navy Theater Wide Area Defense System*, Washington, Department of Defense, March 25, 1996; *Defense News*, April 22, 1996, pp. 12–26, April 29, 1996, p. 3.

158. Secretary of Defense William J. Perry, *Annual Report to the President and the Congress*, Department of Defense, Washington, February 1995, p. 83.

159. *Washington Post*, May 8, 1996; Reuters, May 7, 1996, 1614.

160. Kiya Batmanglidj, "From Russia With Arms: Russian Security Cooperations and the Implications for US Policy," *The Graduate Review, 1995/1996*, Washington, American University, 1996, p. 38.

161. Secretary of Defense William J. Perry, *Annual Report to the President and the Congress, FY1997*, Department of Defense, Washington, February 1996, pp. 56–57; Testimony of Dr. Harold P. Smith, Assistant Secretary of Defense (Nuclear & Chemical, & Biological Defense Programs) to the Strategic Forces Subcommittee of the Senate Armed Services Committee, March 13, 1996; Office of the Secretary of Defense, *Proliferation: Threat and Response*, Washington, Department of Defense, April 1996, pp. 52–55.

162. Secretary of Defense William J. Perry, *Annual Report to the President and the Congress*, Department of Defense, Washington, February 1995, pp. 87–89.

Chapter 9

163. Brigadier General Robert H. Scales, *Certain Victory: The United States Army in the Gulf War*, Washington, Office of the Chief of Staff, US Army, 1993, p. 6.

164. Unclassified US data compound these uncertainties. ACDA reports that Iran imported an average of over $3 billion a year in constant 1993 dollars. It cut these imports to $1.6 billion in 1989, raised them to $2.0 billion in 1990 and $2.2 billion in 1991, cut them to $369 million in 1992, and spent $1 billion in 1993. These data are scarcely an indication of a massive Iranian build-up.

Sources and Methods

This volume is part of a series of volumes on each of the Gulf states which has been developed by the Center for Strategic and International Studies as part of a dynamic net assessment of the Middle East. This project has had the sponsorship of each of the Southern Gulf states as well as US sponsors of the CSIS, and each text has been widely distributed for comment to experts and officials in each Southern Gulf country, to US experts and officials, and to several international agencies and institutions, and various private experts.

Sources

The author has drawn heavily on the inputs of outside reviewers throughout the text. It was agreed with each reviewer, however, that no individual or agency should be attributed at any point in the text except by specific request, and that all data used be attributed to sources that are openly available to the public. The reader should be aware of this in reviewing the footnotes. Only open sources are normally referred to in the text, although the data contained in the analysis has often been extensively modified to reflect expert comment.

There are other aspects of the sources used of which the reader should be aware. It was possible to visit each Southern Gulf states at various times during the preparation of this book and to talk to local officials and experts. Some provided detailed comments on the text. Interviews also took place with experts in the United States, United Kingdom, France, Switzerland and Germany. Portions of the manuscript were circulated for informal review by European officials and diplomats in some cases. Once again, no details regarding such visits or comments are referenced in the text.

Data from open sources are deliberately drawn from a wide range of sources. Virtually all of these sources are at least in partial conflict. There is no consensus over demographic data, budget data, military expenditures and arms transfers, force numbers, unit designations, or weapons types.

While the use of computer data bases allowed some cross-correlation and checking of such source, the reporting on factors like force strengths, unit types and identities, tactics often could not be reconciled and citing multiple sources for each case was not possible because it involved many detailed judgments by the author in reconciling different reports and data.

The Internet and several on-line services were also used extensively. Since such the data bases are dynamic, and change or are deleted over time, there is no clear way to footnote much of this material. Recent press sources are generally cited, but are often only part of the material consulted.

Methods

A broad effort has been made to standardize the analysis of each country, but it became clear early in the project that adopting a standard format did not suit the differences that emerged between countries. The emphasis throughout this phase of the CSIS net assessment has been on analyzing the detailed trends within individual states and this aspects of the analysis has been given priority over country-to-country consistency.

In many cases, the author adjusted the figures and data use in the analysis on a "best guess" basis, drawing on some thirty years of experience in the field. In some other cases, the original data provided by a given source were used without adjustment to ensure comparability, even though this leads to some conflicts in dates, place names, force strengths, etc. within the material presented—particularly between summary tables surveying a number of countries and the best estimates for a specific country in the text. In such cases, it seemed best to provide contradictory estimates to give the reader some idea of the range of uncertainty involved.

Extensive use is made of graphics to allow the reader to easily interpret complex statistical tables and see long-term trends. The graphic program used was deliberately standardized, and kept relatively simple, to allow the material portrayed to be as comparable as possible. Such graphics have the drawback, however, that they often disguise differences in scale and exaggerate or minimize key trends. The reader should carefully examine the scale used in the left-hand axis of each graphs.

Most of the value judgments regarding military effectiveness are made on the basis of American military experience and standards. Although the author has lived in the Middle East, and worked as a US advisor to several Middle Eastern governments, he believes that any attempt to create some Middle Eastern standard of reference is likely to be far more arbitrary than basing such judgments on his own military background.

Mapping and location names presented a major problem. The author used US Army and US Air Force detailed maps, commercial maps, and in some cases commercial satellite photos. In many cases, however, the place names and terrain descriptions used in the combat reporting by both sides, and by independent observers, presented major contradictions that could not be resolved from available maps. No standardization emerged as to the spelling of place names. Sharp differences emerged in the geographic data published by various governments, and in the conflicting methods of transliterating Arabic and Farsi place names into English.

The same problem applied in reconciling the names of organizations and individuals—particularly those being transliterated from Arabic and Farsi. It again became painfully obvious that no progress is being made in reconciling the conflicting methods of transliterating such names into English. A limited effort has been made to standardize the spellings used in this text, but many different spellings are tied to the relational data bases used in preparing the analysis and the preservation of the original spelling is necessary to identify the source and tie it to the transcript of related interviews.

About the Book and Author

This volume provides the first detailed analysis of the trends in U.S. contingency capabilities since the end of the Gulf War, the impact of the Bush administration's "Base Force" policy, and the Clinton administration's "Bottom Up Review" of current U.S. contingency capabilities. It examines U.S. capabilities in the Gulf through the year 2001, the impact of current force improvement plans and defense budgets, and the new problems created by the need for counter-proliferation strategy. Finally, it details the new strategic relationships that have developed between the U.S. and the Southern Gulf states since the Gulf War, as well as the impact of U.S. arms sales and military assistance.

Anthony H. Cordesman has served in senior positions in the office for the secretary of defense, NATO, and the U.S. Senate. He is currently a senior fellow and Co-Director of the Middle East Program at the Center for Strategic and International Studies, an adjunct professor of National Security Studies at Georgetown University, and a special consultant on military affairs for ABC News. He lives in Washington, D.C.